Help...
I'm a
Stepmother

Help...
I'm a
Stepmother

Sonja Ridden

metro

Published by Metro Publishing Ltd, 3 Bramber Court,
2 Bramber Road, London, W14 9PB, England

This edition first published in the UK in 2002

ISBN 1 84358 055 1

British Library Cataloguing-in-Publication Data: A catalogue record for this
book is available from the British Library.

Design by ENVY

Printed and bound in Great Britain by Bookmarque.

1 3 5 7 9 10 8 6 4 2

DEDICATION

This book is dedicated to my two stepsons.
Thank you for allowing me to be your 'mum',
for letting me accompany you on part of your life's journey.
for putting up with me, which I know hasn't always been easy,
for being catalysts for my personal growth and
for teaching me how to love unconditionally.

ACKNOWLEDGEMENTS

*Special thanks go to my long-suffering husband, who was my first
reader, editor and encourager, to my children, who have had to
become very independent over the past few years
(thank heavens they love take-away!)
to Rhondda, Dolores and Cyndi, without whose encouragement
(and helpful input) I might not have had the courage to see
this project through to the end,
to John, my friend and second editor, whose assistance
has been invaluable,
to Kimberly for her great illustrations,
to Renée and Siobhán, my 'real' editors,
to all the clients who have graciously given their permission to be
quoted in this book and last, but by no means least,
to my mother, who has instilled within me my love for writing.*

CONTENTS

ABOUT THE AUTHOR

Sonja Ridden holds a Master of Counselling degree and is a counsellor/psychotherapist in private practice in Sydney. Although she specialises in assisting stepfamilies, her counselling expertise covers a broad range of client issues.

She is also a skilled group facilitator and public speaker on issues relating to stepfamily living and the personal growth and empowerment of women.

Recognising the lack of stepfamily support in Australia, Sonja has recently developed 'The Step Stop', a website dedicated to the provision of resources, education and support for all stepfamily members. Her website also provides links to stepfamily information and services throughout the world; an opportunity to connect with other stepfamilies as well as online support opportunities for stepfamily members to reveal their stories, exchange their knowledge and share their wisdom – a first step for stepfamilies seeking support.

You can find Sonja's website at *www.thestepstop.com* or contact her by e-mailing *sonja@thestepstop.com*

FOREWORD

When Sonja first told me she was writing a book on step-parenting, I was overjoyed. I wished I had such a guide when I remarried seven years ago. When my partner and I first met ten years ago, we each had two children, aged a year apart: 13, 14, 15 and 16. Could our new relationship survive four teenagers?

Like Sonja, I discovered the challenges and rewards of step-parenting in uncharted territory. However, there were many moments when I wished there was a roadmap or a guide to follow. Sonja has provided this roadmap in the form of her book *Help...I'm a Stepmother*, which can be considered a survivor's guide to being a step-parent.

Sonja has written the book from both her personal experience as a step-parent and her professional expertise as a therapist and counsellor. Her journey is written with honesty and courage. Sonja tells how, as a young and in-love

24-year-old immigrant to Australia, she married a man with two small sons. Shortly after they married, the children's mother disappeared, leaving Sonja to be the full-time carer of two distraught and abandoned little boys.

Sonja describes her struggles and triumphs, her pain and growth through her experiences. Most importantly, she explains the process of step-parenting and gives us a deeper understanding of the blended family. She describes the different stages, the emotions to expect and provides us with tools to deal with each phase.

If you are a step-parent or are about to become part of a blended family, this book is a must. Sonja's style is easy to read, her advice is practical and down to earth. Her words offer insight and understanding in a circumstance that is often filled with confusion, hurt and anger. Although mothering often comes to us by instinct, few of us are born with the innate skills of being a step-parent.

This book provides the tools for you to turn this potentially painful experience into a rewarding journey. Effective strategies and case studies are intermingled with Sonja's own personal story. *Help...I'm a Stepmother* is an important contribution to this field as more and more of us have another go at marriage or find ourselves in the role of step-parent.

Cyndi Kaplan-Freiman is the author of nine books, including There's a Lipstick in My Briefcase.

INTRODUCTION

When I said 'I do', I not only acquired a husband but also two little boys, a cat and a goldfish. At the time, although apprehensive, I thought that I had a pretty good idea of what I was about to get myself into. It didn't take me long to discover, however, that the reality was significantly different from my expectations.

Since I was committed to making my marriage work, I began to search frantically for helpful reading material on step-parenting and was eventually rewarded by finding one solitary book on the subject. Delving into it, I soon realised that it would not provide the help I was so desperate to find. Although adept at describing her own step-parenting battle, the author had failed to provide suggestions for avoiding being fatally wounded on the battlefield. Reading her book left me feeling more depressed than I had been before and confirmed my suspicion that the prospects for survival weren't good!

Twenty years later I can confirm from my personal and professional experience that step-parenting is indeed a battle not recommended for the faint-hearted. I can also confirm, however, that there are rewards that make the experience satisfying and worthwhile. The ready availability today of pertinent information also assists in making the stepfamily journey a more hopeful one.

Understanding the dynamics of a stepfamily can go a long way toward helping you 'hang in there' when the going gets tough. The knowledge that other step-parents also struggle with feelings of confusion, anger, isolation, insecurity, resentment and a sense of failure can be invaluable when you find yourself feeling overwhelmed. Being assured that these painful emotions are a normal part of stepfamily living can be a great comfort and encouragement, especially if the assurances are accompanied by practical suggestions. So, whilst stepfamily living seems to be just as difficult today as it was twenty years ago, there is greater access to resources that will help you understand, work at and grow through the experience.

There are many different facets to stepfamily life. However, the major focus of this book is the gamut of feelings that are prevalent in the experiences of most stepfamilies. In order to illustrate the crippling effect these feelings can have on family members and the freedom and personal growth that can be gained as a result of understanding and learning to deal with those emotions, I have chosen to share portions of my own step-parenting journey with you. Although my situation may be quite different from yours, you are no doubt intimately acquainted with many of the feelings that often caused my life to be a misery. The reason I have chosen this focus is that these painful emotions usually accompany the most difficult stages of our step-parenting experience, and frequently are the cause of yet another family separation. It was the hard-won recognition that my 'awful feelings' were normal in my circumstance that not only saved my marriage, my sanity and my self-respect, but also set me on a path to personal development and growth. I have found the same to be true for many clients who have sought my help in their stepfamily struggles.

As I take you on a journey through these emotions you will find many practical suggestions and hints that are the result of much trial and error within my own experience, as well as useful ideas that have been shared with me throughout my years of assisting new and experienced stepmothers and stepfathers. It is my hope that sharing these with you will help you recognise that the confusing and painful emotions with which you may be struggling are a common aspect of the step-parenting experience. They don't last forever and, if you let them, they can become your platform to maturity, growth and the great purpose life has in store for you.

When we long for a life without difficulties, remember that oaks grow strong in contrary winds and diamonds are made under pressure.
PETER MARSHALL

Hep! Im a StepMum!

MY STORY

Austrian by birth and cosmopolitan by nature, I was 24 years of age, footloose and fancy-free when I arrived in Australia. Five years later I found myself back in Austria, exchanging marriage vows. This came about in a whirlwind way as I had travelled back home for a holiday, not expecting to return as a married woman. My partner, an Australian divorcee with two small children, fearing that I might 'slip through the net', thought it a good idea to follow me, propose and make our relationship legal. Thus swept up in the romance of the moment, in love and filled with the vision and the confidence of youth we 'tied the knot'. The ambience of the quaint Austrian village and the snowflakes swirling all around us as we took the step into wedded bliss, added to the magic of the experience.

Reality, however, swiftly caught up with us on our return to Australia. Now my life began as the stepmother of two pre-school-aged boys. With no particular interest in children (in general), nor any previous mothering experience, I felt like I was entering an entirely new world without a compass or a roadmap.

To make matters worse, the children's biological mother, with whom they had previously spent the occasional weekend, decided soon after that 'it was all too hard' and disappeared, it seemed, from the face of the earth. Naturally, the sudden reality of not being able to see their mother, and without understanding why, was very distressing for the boys. While continuing to assure them of her affection, my partner and I were at a loss to explain their mother's disappearance. Little did we know that it would take 14 years before she would reconnect with her children.

Although both boys suffered as a result of their mother's abandonment, one of them seemed almost unable to cope. This child, who, as we discovered many years later, also suffered from severe Attention Deficit Hyperactivity Disorder (ADHD), made family life an extraordinary challenge.

A few years into our marriage my partner and I produced two more boys, whose addition to our lives seemed to normalise our family which had felt so different from all other families I knew. Their presence enabled me to feel more like a 'legitimate' mother. They gave me greater parenting confidence and helped me to feel significantly more comfortable with my situation.

Since to all intents and purposes we were a functioning family unit, few people realised the struggle, the multitude of complex emotions, the anguish and heartache that lay behind the mask of normality. Approximately ten years into my marriage, physically exhausted, emotionally drained and spiritually bankrupt, I discovered that if anything was going to change in my family life experience, the change would have to begin with me. This was a significant realisation, which became the first step on a life-changing journey of self-discovery, personal growth and emotional and spiritual development. Although it was unfamiliar and difficult at first, I soon began to enjoy the new challenge, to revel in its revelations and gratefully discover its benefits to me, my husband and all four of our children. The journey, which has by no means ended, is an exciting and rewarding one. It has helped me become a new person, has given me a life purpose, helped me move into the challenging and worthwhile profession of counselling, and has made me strong and humble, thankful and complete.

Although I would never have chosen this path had I known its hardships and heartaches, I thank God for granting me the privilege of walking it. I thank my husband for his love and unwavering support through all the difficult times. I thank my natural sons for enabling me to discover the many joys of biological motherhood. Last, but by no means least, I thank my stepsons, without whom I would not be on this journey, for all the treasures I was able to find along its difficult path and for teaching me, in the midst of it all, the meaning of unconditional love.

THE STEPFAMILY
LIFE CYCLE

In order to understand the rollercoaster ride of emotions you are likely to experience in step-parenting, it helps to be familiar with the stepfamily life cycle. Taking a look at any stepfamily, we find that it has a life cycle that is very different from that of the traditional family. This is rarely understood at the beginning of our new journey.

Traditionally, couples who decide to travel life's path together have the luxury of time. The individuals are able to get to know each other without having to take responsibility for anyone but themselves. Ideally they will have established a strong couple bond before their first baby arrives on the scene. As they make room for this little one in their lives, their ability to love, share and nurture grows and matures. With each new addition to the family, and through the passage of time, they develop the capacity to deal with the life stages that follow a fairly predictable manner. Babies become toddlers, reach school age, turn into teenagers, leave the family home, find partners and have their own families. Throughout this process, parenting roles are established, beliefs are formed, values are adopted, traditions created and family life takes on a natural rhythm.

Individuals embarking on the stepfamily journey rarely recognise that they will be unable to follow this predictable path. The naturally occurring stages of traditional families resemble more of a jigsaw jumble in step- and blended families. Couples starting their partnership with a number of children of varying ages have little time to get to know each other away from the responsibility, distraction and pressure of these responsibilities. Accommodating new personalities, establishing new roles, incorporating new values and developing new relationships means adjusting to monumental changes. Although different stepfamily experts identify different numbers and stages occurring within the step- and blended family development, I have found the following five (as similarly identified by Newman M. (1994)) to be most helpful:

Fantasy Stage

Most couples who decide to embark on the step-parenting journey do so while they are madly in love and filled with great hopes and dreams. They have the firm belief that no obstacle will be too great for their love to overcome. This is probably why the first step in the stepfamily journey has been dubbed the 'Fantasy Stage'. This stage usually comes to a swift end as the reality of life in the new family structure hits home and we realise that it is not the way we had imagined.

Transition Stage

In this stage we discover that our stepchildren are not the darlings we had been looking forward to embracing and nurturing – by now we might even view them as 'the dreaded enemy'. Our own children may be displaying disturbing signs such as jealousy and resentment, which leave us feeling helpless and guilty. Our partners may be exhausted by their attempts to please us, to 'win over' our children and 'make up' to theirs. We are often caught somewhere in-between, reeling from the chaos and confusion of it all. We could be overwhelmed, swinging between feelings of anger, resentment, insecurity and loneliness. We might be wondering what we have got ourselves into and why – questioning our own sanity. We might feel disappointed, disempowered and inadequate, harbouring the painful suspicion that somehow all of this is our fault. This stage usually is closely followed by the Conflict Stage.

Conflict Stage

This is a stage of conflict and struggle within the stepfamily. By now we have fully recognised that the dreams we had in our Fantasy Stage were just that – dreams. We have also moved to the realisation that everything that isn't working in our stepfamily is not our fault. We are weary of all the turmoil and pain and we are increasingly aware that we too have needs that largely remain unmet. We know that we cannot go on like this. As we struggle to create a more comfortable fit within the stepfamily structure, emotions run high and conflicts are heated. While this usually is the most painful stage of our experience, it is also the pivotal point of our family relationships. Although some couples do decide at this point that 'it's all too hard' and consequently separate, for others it becomes the platform for positive change, leading to the Action Stage.

Action Stage

This is the stage where old ideals are discarded and new family structures are built. Here, important decisions are made about the way we want our relationships to be. We resolve difficult issues and establish workable boundaries for ourselves. Although this stage is one that requires hard work and effort, it is a satisfying and personally empowering one. As we establish specific guidelines for our stepfamily, we begin to feel more in control. The family atmosphere becomes more relaxed, and we feel a greater sense of accomplishment, security and freedom.

Resolution Stage

This is the stage at which the family members finally feel connected and bonded. Even if the bond is not necessarily one of love, it might be one of affection, respect or simply one of familiarity. Family members now know each other, warts and all. Shared history has been created. Difficulties, conflict, laughter and tears have brought all of us closer together. The stepfamily has a life of its own.

Although these stages may appear to be 'cut and dried', let me caution you – they are not! They usually merge one into the other, without coming into our conscious awareness. Some stages take longer in some families than in others and there is no way we can put a time limit on them. Unexpected stress might send us back to an earlier stage, while a prolonged period of peace and harmony or a significant experience of personal growth might move us forward more rapidly. At times we might even seesaw between them. The secret to moving successfully through these stages is to recognise that they are normal. We need to learn to go with the flow, to enjoy the good times and refuse to get stuck in the bad. It also helps to remind ourselves that no stage lasts forever, and that there is a light at the end of the tunnel.

Don't beat yourself up if you don't move as quickly as you would like. Make a point of celebrating every success and there is a good chance that, in the end, you will find that the journey was worthwhile.

BEFORE THE
BIG STEP

When the relationship with the man who was to become my husband took on a serious nature I had no idea that I was going to be an instant mother. Of course, I knew that he had two little boys who were part of the household he was sharing with his mother at the time, but I assumed that the boys' mother would raise the children, as seemed common practice in that era. I had no objections to being a 'fill-in', but had absolutely no wish, intention or desire to be a mother, step- or otherwise. I had a career, a comfortable life and zero maternal instinct. By the time I discovered that the boys' biological mother had even less maternal instinct than I did, retreat, although enormously attractive, seemed no longer an option. I was in too deep! I was in love and also equipped with a very well-developed (in retrospect I would say overly developed) sense of responsibility. Furthermore, it seemed ludicrous to leave a man for the display of the very qualities that had attracted me to him in the first place. So, in keeping with my rather stubborn nature, I gritted my teeth and determined to make this situation work. I had no idea how I was going to achieve this lofty goal, but accepted my mother-in-law's assurance that 'love will overcome all difficulties'.

You too may have been subject to similar words of encouragement. You might have been told things like 'the children will be so grateful to have a new mum', 'the kids can't help but love you', 'don't worry, it'll be no different to a first marriage'. If you are already in a stepfamily situation, you no doubt have discovered that this kind of sentiment has little resemblance to reality. Whilst well-intentioned, it is naïve, idealistic and uttered by someone who clearly has no idea of the stepfamily experience. Unfortunately, these kinds of sentiments can set us up for major disillusionment and disappointment, and can cause us to feel like failures when we realise that we cannot achieve these goals. For those who have not as yet taken the big leap, this chapter will provide a realistic look at the complexities that challenge stepfamilies. For those already in the relationship, it might provide a clue as to why you may find yourselves confused and struggling instead of 'dancing over the hills that are alive with the *Sound of Music*'!

No matter how we look at it, stepmothering is no Sunday picnic – it is difficult, demanding, often frustrating, sometimes heartbreaking and anything but romantic.

Stepping into Stepfamily

The reasons people end up as single parents (the death of or separation/divorce from their partner) usually leave a legacy of pain. The potential step-parent would do well to remember that this legacy not only affects the remaining parent, but also impacts on the children. If at the time of loss the parents are too preoccupied with their own pain to respond to the pain of their children, this can have devastating effects and leave the children with deep emotional scars long after the parent has come to terms with his or her own pain and grief. The unfortunate reality often is that the remaining parent may be too angry and hurt, too depressed or distressed (or just too busy coping) to be fully there for the children, so the step-parent may well be the one who is left to 'pick up the pieces'.

Beginning the step-journey we usually do not know, to any real extent, our new family's legacy of the past. Even if we did, we could not possibly foresee the difficulties that await as its consequences. Each step-situation brings its own unique set of challenges, because no two step- or blended families are totally alike. For example:

- You may, like me, find yourself in the role of 'instant' mother (add husband, kids and stir).
- You may be bringing children of your own into a relationship with a person who has never been a parent.
- You may both have a number of children from one or more previous marriages.
- You may have a partner whose children are grown up and flit in and out of your life.
- Your own children may be adults, while your partner's children are still at an age where they require parenting.
- You may be a full-time carer to both your own and your partner's children, or be an 'access' parent to either or both sets of children.
- There may be a significant age difference between you and your partner, which may make him or her less inclined to have more children, while you may be desperate to create a family together.

Recognising the complexity of the stepfamily reality, it is clear that there is no simple formula for success. It is helpful to realise that all step- and blended family situations, no matter how diverse, have one thing in common — one or more hurting children. Although the break-up of the family, be it due to separation or death, leaves no child unscathed, the degree of emotional impact may vary significantly from child to child and from situation to situation. How their pain is displayed and/or dealt with depends very much on the child's disposition and the skill with which it is handled by the important people in his or her life. Whether they have grandparents, uncles, aunts or perhaps a supportive teacher, scouts or church leader, will play an important role in how the children handle the situation.

Exploring the 'Baggage'

The important issue for you to remember when you accept the step-parenting job is that you are entering into relationship with not just one person but a number of people. All these people bring with them their personal history as well as historical connections that you do not share. They all have experienced a significant and painful event – the loss of a partner or a parent. This, of necessity, has an impact on the life you are planning to begin together. Most of us carry through our lives memories, or 'baggage', of what we experience along the way. Although your new relationship represents the beginning of a new journey, each person in the stepfamily has some 'baggage' that they bring along for the ride. Depending on your life history, you may have one or a number of 'bags' of varying sizes and weights. Some may be bulging with romantic fantasies, others might enclose your hopes and fears, some may contain loads of expectations, while still others could be filled with grief,

sadness, shame, guilt, secrets you've never told – in short, all the things of your past. Your partner also brings along his or her baggage. The number of the pieces he or she carries, their size and weight depend on his or her life experiences.

Ordinarily when couples join together they spend time exploring each other's baggage, shed some along the way and decide to carry the rest together. When you enter a step- or blended family situation you decide to journey with people who already have a great deal of baggage which they have trouble carrying on their own. Their bags may be huge, they could be excessively heavy and worst of all, you may not even know what is contained within them. So, before you know it, you might find yourself buckling under the weight of your own bags which are squashed beneath the additional burden you have taken on. This scenario shows how important it is to ensure that your own bags are manageable before you try to carry someone else's load. The heavier your own bag of hurts, unmet needs and unfinished business of the past, the less likely your success in step-parenting. Therefore, it is very important to make a good attempt to sort out any difficulties and unfinished business from your past **before** considering the big step into stepfamily living.

If you begin your new journey feeling grounded, confident and prepared to tackle any challenge, you will be in a much better position to enjoy the forthcoming task. Equally, its success will be enhanced if you are:

- strongly committed to the relationship
- undaunted by the expectation that it won't be 'a bed of roses'
- strengthened by the knowledge that nothing worthwhile comes easily
- spurred on by the understanding that it's the difficulties in life that facilitate maturity and personal growth
- unafraid to take a good look at reality.

Reality is ...

- Your stepchildren are not the ones who have chosen you.
- You cannot ever replace the children's biological parent.
- The children may not like you.
- You may not like the children.
- The children may regard it as their most noble task to drive you and your partner apart.

- The children may compare you unfavourably with their biological parent.
- The children may be resentful at having to share the attention and affection of their mum or dad.
- The children may be unresponsive to your attempts at creating an emotional connection with them.
- The children may be hurting badly and behave accordingly. They could be:
  − distressed
  − naughty
  − emotionally disturbed
  − destructive of self and/or others.
- Your honeymoon may never occur. Alternatively, it may include one or more (not so optional) extras.
- You need to share your partner's time, attention and love right from the start of your relationship.
- If you weren't a parent before becoming a step-parent, you'll never experience the joys of having your very first baby together, the exhilaration of bringing into your lives a new little person or the luxury of adjusting your time and emotional clock to the demands of a new baby.
- You cannot learn and grow with your child through the stages from newborn baby to toddler and so on, because while your child is experiencing these stages you also have to care for children at different stages of development.
- You may be called upon to do many things you would not ordinarily choose to do, such as becoming a 'tuckshop mum' or getting up in the middle of the night to soothe a frightened child.

In a situation where you have brought your own children into the relationship there is a possibility of:

- resentment between your own and your partner's children
- jealousy and fighting
- verbal, emotional and physical (in some cases even sexual) abuse*
- differences in values, beliefs and expectations
- stepchildren's role-modelling of what you consider undesirable and inappropriate behaviour, which can affect your own children
- difficulty in exercising fairness in the way you treat your own children versus your stepchildren. This is a particularly difficult issue if you dislike your stepchildren.

Don't be discouraged by this — remember, forewarned is forearmed! If you go into the experience knowing what to expect, reality won't come as quite such a rude shock and won't have the same power to throw you off balance. Depending on your situation the reality you are facing may have many aspects (including aspects of a positive nature) that you will not find listed here. Here are some positives to keep in mind:

- If you are unable to have children of your own, acquiring a gaggle of stepkids could fill a painful void in your life.
- In some cases, stepchildren really welcome their parent's new partner — you could be one of those lucky ones!

- You may be a much better parent to your stepchildren than your partner's 'ex'. Remember, chances are that one day your stepchildren will appreciate this.
- Your natural children and stepchildren may get on famously.
- The addition of stepchildren may fulfill your lifelong dream of having a big family.

Look for the positives in your particular situation and celebrate!

HINTS

- Face the realities mentioned in this chapter, and accept the possibility that some or all of these, and perhaps more, may be applicable to your situation.
- Share your concerns and fears with your partner.
- Spend as much time as possible with your potential stepfamily before you set up house together.
- Get to know your stepchildren (warts and all).
- Allow them to gain a realistic picture of you and your children (warts and all).
- Give some thought to how you would best deal with your stepchildren's dislike, rejection, resentment of you and/or your children.
- Consider how you will cope if you or your biological children dislike, resent or reject your stepchildren.

- Prepare emotionally for battle and stock up on 'weapons' of understanding, acceptance and kindness.
- Ensure that you have someone who supports you in your new role.

* Abuse of any kind is destructive and should not be tolerated. If you find yourself in an abusive environment and/or discover your children and/or stepchildren to be the victims of abuse, seeking help is essential. Professional assistance is equally crucial if it is you who struggles with abusive impulses. Organisations that are equipped to help you in such circumstances are listed in the Helpful Services section at the end of this book.

TRANSITION

Once I was a stepmother, life became very complicated. Up to that point I had known exactly where I fitted into the social structure. I was single, pursuing a career and mostly enjoying stimulating relationships with people of a similar life status. Suddenly, I found myself married with a three-year-old and a four-year-old who went to pre-school. Joining the huddle of mothers blissfully discussing the latest achievements of their 'little angels' was uncomfortable. I had nothing to contribute, and felt rather out of place. When the conversation turned to the women's various experiences in the labour ward I really started to fidget and soon found that escape was the only option.

I didn't fit in. I had lost my place. I was no longer single, but didn't belong to the group of newlyweds who were either enjoying each other's company or were busy 'trying' for a baby. The world of young marrieds with a baby was totally closed to me and I had no desire at that stage to spend hours discussing the virtues of cloth nappies — as opposed to disposable ones. I had little in common with those mothers huddling together at the pre-school. Having decided that the boys deserved a full-time mother, I had quit my job. Suddenly devoid of the work routine I had enjoyed and stripped of the self-worth and esteem that were its by-products, my life soon became boring and unsatisfying.

It is an accepted fact that any change in life–status (that is, marriage, divorce, the birth of a baby, children leaving home etc.) causes a certain amount of stress. Moving into a stepmothering role represents a major life-change. So it is not surprising that this move is accompanied by an undue amount of stress. If around the same time we are leaving behind a satisfying career (usually an important part of our identity) this can have an unbalancing effect and can increase the stress factor significantly if the stepmothering job represents our first parenting experience. We might feel insecure, anxious and unsure of our ability to cope. Our

feelings of self-worth and esteem might receive a battering. While this is a perfectly normal response to the enormous change in our lives, if it is combined with prolonged feelings of boredom, dissatisfaction and loneliness, it can become the catalyst for a rapid slide into depression. Therefore, it is important that we recognise stress-overload early and learn to manage it. Stress and depression are discussed in further detail in a later chapter.

Things to Consider

- Taking on a partner with kids (a package deal) is no easy feat. Even if you think you know what to expect, be aware that many surprises lurk around every corner and can destabilise your sense of being in control. If you decide at the same time to make another major change such as leaving your job, you might soon find yourself in an identity vacuum. Until now your job has probably been the main focus of your adult life.

- The transition into stepfamily life is usually less traumatic for people who have children already. They have some idea of what to expect in the parenting department. These mothers have, in most cases, also dealt with the issues that arise as a consequence of changing their career. However, they face the additional challenge of blending two sets of children – which is fertile ground for a multitude of difficulties.

- Setting up house with a partner whose children are grown up brings its own complications. Becoming the step-parent of children who are of a similar age to oneself can be a daunting prospect, especially if the children show signs of hostility. Even if these offspring are adults with their own lives, they still hold the power to make a step-parent's life a misery.

- Another difficulty might occur if you are significantly younger than your partner and are hoping to create a new family. Your partner may have adult children and he or she may feel that all the parenting they ever wanted to do has been done, whilst you may be desperate to have a baby together. If not discussed and agreed from the outset, this can cause much frustration, resentment and heartache, and can spell doom to your relationship.

Common Transition Pains

Common transition pains clients have shared with me include:

LONELINESS

When I became a stepmum my single friendships just sort of fizzled out. My old friends were living in a totally different sphere – like in another world. When they wanted to go 'out on the town' could I go along? No! It didn't matter what I wanted to do, I had to think about his kids. I couldn't make a move without finding a babysitter first. It all seemed too hard and I just sort of gave up.

Sue

SHAME

I couldn't tell people that I was a stepmother. It just made me feel like I was second best. Maybe people would think that I was crazy to have taken on a man with kids, that I was desperate or had been 'left on the shelf'. So I pretended that all the kids were mine. Boy, did that sometimes get me into hot water. I remember being caught out at the doctor's surgery when he asked me about Cindy's immunisation history. Of course I had absolutely no idea. I was so embarrassed, I just wanted to crawl under the carpet.

Rita

DIFFICULTIES FORMING RELATIONSHIPS

I just never knew when to tell people that the kids were my stepchildren. It seemed like such a hassle – going through the story time and again. I just couldn't be bothered. It wasn't really anyone else's business anyway. But that sure made it hard to make new friends. Try telling someone when you might have known them for a while – then it seems like you are confessing this huge secret – how embarrassing! It was so awkward and stopped me from making the effort time and again. It seems stupid when I think about it now, but it was a real problem for me at the time.

Jenny

DISILLUSIONMENT

I had no idea it was going to be like this. I feel like I have to make an appointment with Sarah whenever I want a moment with her. She's always busy. If it isn't her work, it's the house, the cooking, the kids. Everything seems to be more important than me — especially the kids. We can't even go out because she says she can't leave them at night. The whole thing is impossible. I am not even sure I love her any more.

Evan

JEALOUSY

I can't stand it! My stepdaughter jumps into my Jim's arms the moment he walks through the door and then she clings to him like ivy for the rest of the night. She pushes between us when I try to kiss him hello and I barely get a word in until she goes to bed. Even then she carries on like a treat if he doesn't sit on her bed until she is asleep. Why does he have to put her before me all the time? I know it's ridiculous, but I am so jealous I could burst.

Anita

HELPLESSNESS

At first I didn't know what hit me. Coming home after work was a nightmare — the house looked like a tornado had swept through it — the kids were at each others' throats, Amy usually was a blubbering mess ... and I was supposed to sort it all out. Why me? What could I do to fix the whole mess?

Brad

UNCERTAINTY

I've never known anyone to lose their temper and be as abusive as Sandra (his ex). It was terrifying and not just because of the distasteful scenes. It really undermined our fairly new relationship. It made me question if we'd moved in together too soon. Was Stewart sure he wanted me despite all the difficulties? Would Jack (his small son) be permanently harmed by all the lies she told him or by our explosive meetings? Not exactly the romantic courtship I'd envisaged!

Karen

LACK OF CONTROL

Being a step-dad wouldn't be so bad if it wasn't for Bob (biological father). Just as we settle into a bit of a routine and have some semblance of normality the kids have to visit with their father ... and you should see them when they come back. They are unrecognisable – rebellious, rude, hyper ... totally spun out. I can't imagine what he does with them, but it better stop ... soon ... for all our sakes.

Ryan

RAGE

Every time I imagine my partner's 'ex' all I feel is cold rage. She is swanning around footloose and fancy free while I am picking up the pieces with Fred and the kids. When I think of her enjoying her freedom and here I am slaving over a hot stove, I just see red. I feel like punching her, scratching her eyes out, wringing her scrawny neck. But who can I tell? Fred's not too happy about the situation either and other people might think I am dangerous. Maybe I am – I sure feel like it at times!

Carole

COMMITMENT

Boy, did I live in a dream world! I was filled with such good intentions, but I had absolutely no idea how hard it is. His kids are just awful. They are hostile, offensive and they don't get along with me or with my girls. It feels like I've tried everything, but nothing seems to work. They only acknowledge me if they need me for something. They fight all day long and my girls are frightened of them. I am really not sure if I can last much longer.

Verena

As most women who have had the experience of giving birth know all too well, transition is the painful and confusing stage at which their greatest desire is to leap off the labour bed, tell the prospective father and anyone else who would listen that 'this whole thing is a big mistake' and 'I just want to go home – RIGHT NOW!'

Whilst the physical pain of labour obviously is unique to women, the partner who is present throughout this ordeal often shares her emotional turmoil and may also experience an urge to escape. Similarly, he can find the transition to stepparenting just as harrowing (as expressed in some of the above examples).

The transition from your former life into stepfamily living

can be just as emotional and confusing. When little Johnny refuses to eat the slimy green things (the culinary delight you have created especially for him), when Janet screams at the top of her lungs 'You can't tell me what to do, you are not my real father and I hate you!' and Sally engages her dad in a deep and meaningful conversation while ignoring you completely, you'll be wondering whether you should have your head examined for remaining in this relationship. When you find yourself vacillating between the determination to see this through (to the end) and the desire to 'run for the hills', it helps to remember that this stage won't last for ever. The new situation, which may feel desperately un-comfortable right now, will in time become more familiar and less difficult. When little Johnny gives you his first spontaneous hug, teenager Janet thinks you are 'really cool' and adult stepchild Sally actually takes your advice, you will think step-parenting is rewarding and wonder what all the fuss has been about.

HINTS

- Remember that it is normal to feel transition pains.
- Don't make too many changes at once.
- You cannot be all things to all people – so don't even try.
- Don't take the children's responses personally.
- Remember that the transition phase will pass.
- Be kind to

EXPECTATIONS

Having accustomed myself to the idea of full-time step-parenting, my aim was to be a wonderful mother. In fact, I was planning to be the best mother anyone could ever wish to have. I wanted to make up to the boys what they had missed out on. I was going to love and nurture them, teach them, have them spick and span, well behaved and polite. I was intending to bake the best biscuits, cook the most nutritious meals, play with them, help out at their school — in short I was going to be supermum! Well it wasn't long before I realised that my struggle was all uphill. The more perfect I wanted things to be, the worse they seemed to get. My picture-book image of sitting in front of the open fire, reading sugar plum stories to red-cheeked children contentedly snuggled against my knees was shattered almost immediately. Instead, our home resembled a war zone most of the time.

The move into stepfamily living can set us up for a multitude of false expectations. Although I felt it appropriate in my situation to embrace the mothering role fully, my image of how a mother should be was more than a little unrealistic. It's not just the false expectations we might have of ourselves that cause us unnecessary misery. Some expectations we place on our partners and indeed our stepchildren may be just as unrealistic, and have the potential to doom our new relationship to rapid failure.

Whilst expectations can have a thousand different faces, some expectations relating to yourself could be:

- I am going to be such a terrific parent, the children won't even miss their real mum.
- Of course I am going to love the kids; after all, I love their dad.
- I must always put my new family's well-being before my own.
- If I get angry with my partner or his children, it means I am failing in my new role.
- I'll be a better partner and a much better parent than his 'ex'.
- I can take anything the kids dish up.

Some expectations relating to your partner could be:

- I must always be understood by him.
- It's his job to make me happy.
- He is responsible for his kids' behaviour.

- If he doesn't support me 100 per cent in my new role it means that he doesn't love me.
- I must come first. His children don't matter as much as I do.
- The kids won't ever come between us.

Some expectations relating to your stepchildren could be:

- The kids should be thankful that I came into their lives.
- Of course they'll love me; after all, their dad loves me.
- They should appreciate me.
- They should not be jealous of my relationship with their father.
- They have no reason to be angry, upset or annoyed with me. If they are, they only have themselves to blame.
- They had better accept my way of doing things because I am their new mum.

(Although the expectations I've listed are expressed from the perspective of the stepmother, they can be equally true for stepfathers.)

One of the most important things to recognise about unrealistic expectations is that we all have some and that having them neither means that we are selfish nor that we are ignorant. Our expectations usually arise from our hopes, dreams and secret desires. They can be birthed by unfulfilled wishes and/or needs of our past. They can be our cherished dream of creating a better, healthier and more satisfying future for our new families. Unrealistic expectations have the potential to become a big problem, however, if we are unwilling or unable to discuss, challenge or 'reality check' them. When these expectations are brought out into the open we quickly realise that they may need to be modified or even discarded. Keeping them a secret can cause much disappointment and heartache, and may cause our new relationship to flounder even before it has a chance to develop.

The boys, who were like chalk and cheese, fought about everything. If it wasn't over a toy, they'd squabble over who would sit in the front seat of the car, who could run faster, spit further, shout louder or over what would be watched on TV. They'd argue and fight, scream and shout, kick and punch each other. Without any parenting experience to fall back on, I was horrified by this. My nervous costume soon hung in unglamorous tatters. However, I was determined to conquer this by hook or by crook. Let me confess, I succeeded in nothing more than making matters worse. I became judge and jury in war games that were never meant to be won. No wonder I wasn't particularly popular, and I was worn out at the end of each exhausting day.

Full-Time Step-Parenting

Parenting is a difficult task in the best of circumstances. It is even more difficult in a step-situation. If you are a first-time parent, I encourage you to find out what kind of behaviour is appropriate for the age/s of your stepchildren. Studying some 'how to' parenting material might be a first step in getting a handle on the situation. Joining a parenting course will not only help you gain a more balanced view of the kind of behaviour that is appropriate for your stepchildren, it will also connect you with other parents. Last but not least, it helps to remember that, even in traditional families, siblings squabble and fight. Don't expect to become an experienced parent overnight. Don't expect to become a perfect parent – ever!

If you are a seasoned parent already, don't be surprised or discouraged if your stepchildren don't respond to you in the same way as your own children. The expectations placed on your stepchildren's behaviour in their original (or other) home might be very different – their values and beliefs perhaps diametrically opposed to yours, as Sally illustrates: 'The kids storm in – they don't even say "hello". Then they strew around all their stuff. Everywhere I go, I find their bits and pieces. When I go off my head at them, they act surprised'. As Sally discovered when, in desperation, she talked this over with her partner, the kids didn't just act surprised, they were surprised. Politeness and neatness aren't issues in their biological mother's home, so they simply weren't aware that these are things of importance to their stepmother. When Sally and the children's father make their expectations of behaviour clear to the children, they can then reasonably expect the beginnings of change.

Andrea told me with a degree of frustration: 'My step-kids jump up the moment they've finished their meal and race off to do their own thing. They don't even bother to ask if they can be excused. I can't stand it! They just leave me sitting there all on my own. It's the epitome of rudeness!' It helped Andrea when she was reminded that after the children's biological mother's death, mealtime etiquette was not an issue of particular importance. With a little sensitivity and patience her stepchildren became accustomed to most of the things Andrea considered vital to smooth family functioning.

The Working Step-Parent

Being a 21st-century parent, you may choose work instead of the full-time parenting option, and this may prove a more sensible and satisfying choice. Neither you nor your stepchildren are well served if you become a stay-at-home parent when everything within you screams for your work environment. Although balancing your job with parenting might prove challenging, it could be the very thing that keeps you sane. What needs to be remembered in such a case is that if your stepchildren are pre-school age this option requires childminding solutions that could be costly. Nannies aren't cheap! Finding a childminding centre that will look after your stepcharges while you are at work may be difficult. Encouraging your partner to give up his or her job could be an option if you hold the kind of job that makes it financially possible for you to support the family. Willing relatives, I've been told, aren't so easy to find these days. However, where there is a will there is a way! If neither full-time parenting nor full-time working feels like a good solution, part-time work might be just the right thing for you. Explore your options and do what feels right for you!

The Weekend Step-Parent

The struggle for step-parents who see their stepchildren only on weekends (partners of non-custodial parents) is often centred on coming to terms with having to share their home, partner and time with (possibly) unwelcome house guests. If they were unprepared for the reality of this weekly, fortnightly or monthly 'intrusion', accepting it as a routine part of their new life may present a particularly difficult challenge. This could become a bigger problem if the step-parent is unable to let their partner know how they feel, as Richard discovered:

> *Evelyn lives for the weekends when her kids come to stay. She plots and plans for days all the things we are going to do together. She gets so excited, I just don't have the heart to tell her that this is really getting to me. I hardly know the kids and I feel a bit like a useless accessory. I'd much rather stay at home and catch up on everything I never get around to doing.*

Step-parents who regard the weekends to be their recovery time after a busy week at work are often less than delighted if they are now called upon to cook for, care for or entertain a number of children whom they barely know and perhaps do not even like. If the children aren't particularly fond of their newly acquired stepmum or dad either, the weekend scenario could be a recipe for disaster. What may have looked like a small hurdle at the outset could swiftly turn into a rather large mountain. Sylvene reports:

> *When his kids come around, all I feel is used and abused. I tried so hard in the beginning. I'd cook up a storm, prepare*

*for stuff to do and really put myself out for them. But all
they'd do is whinge, moan and complain about everything.
I'd be a complete wreck by Monday — and for what? It just
isn't worth it. Nowadays they mostly ignore me anyway. I
can't imagine that Guy's so blind to their rotten behaviour.
Telling him is no good though — all that does is cause
hellish rows — and I've had quite enough of those. Truth is
that I don't like his monsters — I'm exhausted and I've just
about had enough of it all.*

As with other stepfamily concerns, communication is an
absolute 'must' in such situations. If you feel unable to adjust
to the new circumstance and you find that your step-
parenting role causes you ongoing grief, it is essential that
you let your partner know. Because this issue can be a rather
delicate matter (as illustrated by the above examples), there is
wisdom in choosing the mood, time and tone of your
discussion with great care. Only once you have shared your
dilemma will you be able to set about finding a workable
solution with your partner. Richard and Evelyn found, after
Richard realised that confession was no longer avoidable, that
the answer was in her spending every alternate weekend visit
alone with her children. She soon realised that this solution
worked best for them all. She no longer felt as though she
had to please her partner as well as her children. The children
were thrilled to have her to themselves. Richard enjoyed the
time on his own — so everyone was happy.

Whilst this proved to be the answer to Richard and
Evelyn's problem, it may not be right for you. If that is the

case, don't 'throw in the towel' – instead, allow your 'creative juices' to flow and trust that there is a solution that will work for you. Whatever your ultimate decision may be, however, ensure that it is agreeable to you both.

HINTS

- Don't be too hard on yourself.
- Remember that it takes time to adjust to your new role of step-parent.
- Find out about age-appropriate behaviour.
- Kids will be kids – don't expect them to behave like adults.
- Study good parenting books.
- Join a parenting course.
- Find a mentor (someone whose parenting skills you admire).
- Create a peaceful space for yourself (your bedroom, study or any other area where you can have some privacy).
- Don't get involved in your children's battles (unless there is real danger).
- Choose the parenting option that suits your personality and needs.

If you are a weekend-only step-parent and find this role a difficult one, remember:

- Communicating your concerns to your partner is a 'MUST'.
- Be creative in seeking a solution to your dilemma.
- Ensure that the solution suits both you and your partner.

Remember that you can only be as kind to the children as you are to yourself – therefore make time to reward and nurture yourself.

STEPPING INTO THE
CHILDREN'S SHOES

I was baffled, annoyed and hurt by the way one of my stepsons reacted every time I attempted to get close to him or comfort him. His face screwed into a mask of angry determination, his body tense and rigid, it felt like I was trying to embrace a porcupine. I had no idea of what was going on in this child's head or heart and little understanding of what his real needs might be. New to mothering, ignorant of the psychology of a child, unsure of my position and role, I took his response as a sign of personal rejection.

In order to understand what it might be like for your stepchildren, it is important to recognise that children who come from broken homes often struggle with issues of rejection and abandonment. Small children are not able to express their pain verbally, so they find other outlets for the horrible feelings they neither like nor comprehend. They might cry and whine, become aloof and distant, wet the bed, steal, lie, run away, hurt other children and/or hurt themselves. Older children may fall behind in their schoolwork, feel depressed, over-anxious and highly stressed, chew their nails to the elbow, lie awake all night, destroy their own or other people's property, take unusual risks, display suicidal tendencies or show their misery in one of a thousand other ways.

Children whose homes are breaking apart are children in crisis, and desperately need help. Unfortunately, parents in the throes of separation are rarely able to consider fully the needs of their children at such an emotional time. Often, they are barely able to keep their own sanity, much less concern themselves with the emotional stability of their children. 'Kids are resilient', they might reason, and indeed they are. But little hearts break just as easily as big hearts, and the wound of their heartbreak can be so deep that it might take a lifetime to heal.

There are 101 good reasons parents decide to separate. All the children know, however, is that one of their parents is now gone and the remaining one is short-fused, sad and emotionally absent. No sooner have the children adjusted to this new state of affairs when someone else arrives on the scene; someone they don't know and perhaps don't like; whom they didn't invite into their homes or their lives; who threatens the precarious balance they had just begun to find; and who might even have the audacity to try and replace the parent for whom they are still pining. Every time they look at their new step-parent all they can see is the horrible image of a person who is hindering their real parent from coming back to them. And, as if this is not bad enough, it gets even worse if this new and unwanted addition to the household is accompanied by children of his or her own. Not only do the children have to contend with sharing their home, but now they also have to share their remaining parent's time, love and attention.

It took many years until I had the knowledge and understanding to realise what had really been going on for my stepson. It wasn't that he was rejecting me; he was rejecting what was happening to him. His whole life had been turned upside down. Everything that had made up his little world had changed – his biological mother had disappeared from his life, his home had vanished – nothing was the same. It was too much for him to take. He was confused, distressed and angry. In addition, he was suffering from other problems that made his and our lives a misery (covered in a later chapter, see pages 134–8).

As you are seeking to meet your stepchildren's needs, it helps to remember that the basic needs of children are the same the world over. These needs, however, are magnified in children who are grieving the loss of a parent. Even if your stepchildren only visit at access times, an awareness of their needs may function as a roadmap on your step-parenting journey.

Children's needs are as follows:
- Their physical needs are for security, food, shelter and medical care.

- Their emotional needs are to feel wanted, valued, important, respected, special, needed and loved.
- Their intellectual needs are to be given the opportunity for an education and to be taught how to think independently.
- Their spiritual need is for exposure to a workable life philosophy.

How can you best meet these needs?

Witness Protection
Program # 7452

Physical Needs

Children feel secure when they have a 'safe' place. Whilst this can be their old family home, remember that this is a place usually filled with memories of the first family. It may be wiser to start stepfamily life in a home that is new to all members. Providing children with their own room, if at all possible, is thought to be ideal. However, if there is more than one child and they have shared a room in the past, it may help them to share a room together in their new environment. Enable the children to surround themselves with familiar things – perhaps special toy friends, a well-loved blanket or cushion – that can provide them with a feeling of continuity.

Older stepchildren probably wouldn't want to be seen dead with their favourite stuffed animal, but they too have needs for safety, security and continuity. Adult stepchildren also require sensitivity and understanding at this delicate point of separation from the old and commencement of the new. It goes without saying that children can only feel safe and secure in a non-violent environment – one in which they do not feel threatened. They need to be fed healthy and balanced meals, and must have access to medical treatment if they are sick.

Emotional Needs

The need to belong is one of the most pressing human needs. The security of their belonging is particularly threatened in children whose parents' separation has been a bitter one. Battles over 'who gets the kids', where they should live, how often they get to see the non-custodial parent, can destabilise children's sense of belonging even further. Parents who spew hatred at each other and/or involve the children in their battles, or parents who demean each other, can cause significant confusion and damage to their children. No matter how one former partner may feel about the other, children's minds should never be poisoned against them. Children should be allowed to feel good about each of their parents, and should ideally be welcomed warmly and freely in both households.

The need to feel valued is equally important. Children of divorced parents must know that they continue to hold a special place in each parent's heart. This is best demonstrated by spending time with them. Although telling them how special, significant and precious they are is vital, children of all ages understand the language of time much better than words. Being physically and emotionally available to your children, even after divorce has made daily contact impossible, will help them know how important they are to you.

The need to feel loved is a child's greatest emotional need. Expressing love in a way that a child can understand is no easy matter. Expressing love to someone who behaves in a resentful, hostile or rejecting manner can be particularly difficult. Whilst I do not advocate acceptance of abusive behaviour of any kind, I do believe that, especially in the initial stages, certain allowances may need to be made. A large potion of kindness, a positive attitude, elephant skin and a good sense of humour are very helpful at this time.

In order to create a loving, or at least functional, relationship it helps to:	**This says to the child:**
• Give the child time and attention.	'You are important to me. I want to be with you.'
• Treat the child with respect.	'You are a worthwhile person.'
• Listen to, hear and attempt to understand the child.	'What you say has significance, even if I don't agree.'
• Give the child firm guidelines.	'I care for you.'
• Guide and discipline the child in appropriate ways.	'It's important that you learn to fit into the family unit – this is your foundation for life.'
• Allow the child to express her or his feelings.	'I am interested to know how you feel.'
• Refrain from judging the child.	'It's okay to make mistakes.'
• Demonstrate your interest (never ridicule the child).	'I respect your point of view.'
• Establish the facts (do not point the finger of blame at the child).	'You are given the benefit of the doubt … and it's okay to own up.'

It is important that you treat your stepchildren in the same manner as you treat your biological children. Both deserve to receive the same message that it's okay for them to be who they are. All young children are dependent, vulnerable, immature and imperfect, and children who are working through the trauma of separation or loss are even more so. This does not make them worth less than other children; it simply means that they need more affirmation, more care, more love – more of everything!

I am not suggesting that this is an easy task. Adopting this behaviour in ordinary parenting is challenging enough, so adopting it in step-parenting is extraordinarily difficult. The outcome, however, will make your efforts truly worthwhile.

For stepchildren, the experience of moving into a brand-new family situation can be as though the rug has been pulled out from under their feet. They may struggle with a sense of confusion and displacement, and be torn in their loyalties and between feelings of love and hate for the parent whom they perceive is at fault for their dilemmas. They might lose their sense of identity and belonging, and for what can feel like a significant period of time, they might be in a crippling state of limbo.

Being aware of this possibility and understanding that they might actually feel worse than you do may help you to remain loving and kind, even in the face of open dislike, resentment and hostility. Requiring civil behaviour and reasonable participation in as many family activities as possible whilst respecting their need for space gives stepchildren an opportunity to discover where they 'fit'.

Intellectual Needs

Your stepchildren ought to be given the same opportunity for learning as you are willing to give your biological children. The question of private or public school education obviously depends upon your financial means and the agreement of all concerned. If your stepchildren visit only at access times, your influence on their learning will be limited accordingly. Children learn by example, so you can educate them through appropriate role modelling. You may be able to use your times together as opportunities to teach your stepchildren how to think independently. This can be done by involving them in your conversations, by asking their opinions and showing respect for what they think, even if you do not agree with their ideas. Telling children about your mistakes (at an age-appropriate level) can also be a great learning tool. Brainstorming together for better ways of doing things shows them how much you value their input and at the same time lets them know that you do not lay claim to personal perfection. This not only helps the bonding process, but also opens the door for their own confessions. All of this requires time and effort, but it is a wonderful gift to give your stepchildren and is more likely to create secure adults who have faith in their own judgment.

Spiritual Needs

It is important to respect your stepchildren's spiritual beliefs, whatever they may be and whether or not you agree or approve of them. Supporting the continuation of their spiritual journey may prove to be the cementing agent to your relationship. Visits together to spiritual events of their choice can provide an opportunity for warm communication and the building of shared experiences.

If you are aware of your stepchildren's needs and have an honest desire to fulfill them to the best of your ability, you are in a good position to create a happy and functional stepfamily.

HINTS

- Remember that your stepchildren have been through traumatic experiences.
- Give thought to your stepchildren's needs.
- Make your best attempt to meet your stepchildren's needs.

I'M A FAILURE

During my first few years as a step-parent I was desperately unhappy, feeling trapped and unable to cope with the demands of mothering two small boys, one of whom displayed incredibly difficult behaviour. My life seemed like a nightmare from which I couldn't wake, no matter how hard I tried.

The fact that this child had severe problems due to Attention Deficit Hyperactivity Disorder★ (ADHD), a disorder which at that time I didn't even know existed, did not help matters. I was desperately lonely. Attempting to share my pain and frustration with the few who knew the reality of my life was distressing, as they simply didn't understand. How could they? This left me feeling even more lonely, agonisingly inadequate and flooded with shame. I felt like I was a failure.

Failure is a painful experience, and thus fear of failure ranks high on the fear scale. In a society that measures worth by

levels of success, failure immediately creates images of worthlessness, not being good enough or not measuring up to someone else's expectations or standards. This fear triggers painful hidden memories in most people. For some, the experience of failure is connected with being shamed by important people in their lives. Having been the brunt of a cruel joke or the target of ridicule often leaves significant scars. Shaming school experiences also play a big part in the terror that accompanies our fear of failure. Nobody likes to fail!

As stepmothers it is easy to make the mistake of comparing our experience with that of biological mothers; this can throw us into agonising feelings of inferiority. Mothering and stepmothering cannot, reasonably, be compared. Biological mothers have the benefit of carrying their 'bundle of joy' for nine months, and go through the birth experience which (normally) is a powerful bonding agent. Hormones surge and love overwhelms the new mother as she suckles the tiny creature who adoringly gazes into her eyes. She is there to enjoy her baby's first crooked grin, watch the first stumbling steps, band-aid the first bloody knee. She knew her child in its total dependence and innocence and, in most cases, has many years of shared experiences with him or her. By the time you (their stepmother) arrive on the scene, the tiny, innocent and delightful little creature has usually turned into something much less captivating and attractive, which makes the child more difficult to like. Your stepchild may not accept you readily, either. Nothing works the way you had envisaged – and bingo, you have a perfect recipe for a sense of failure.

Some stepmothers have expressed their feelings of failure to me as follows:

I can't do anything right for my stepkids. No matter what I do or how hard I try, they always tell me that their mum does it this way or that, and of course her way is always better than mine.'

Sandy

I'm really not a very good mother. Yes, I do everything for them, but I resent every minute of it. I can't imagine that I will ever love them.
Rebekka

I just can't handle his kids. When he is around things aren't too bad, but as soon as he turns his back its bedlam. I have no power, no control, no authority. I feel helpless and it frustrates me that I can't deal with them.
Ruth

I thought that I would make a difference in their lives, but I am so hopeless that I can't even be a proper mother to them. They don't want me. They don't even like me. I am such a failure.
Jillian

Feeling like a failure in the step-parenting arena is not unique to stepmothers; some stepfathers have voiced their feelings as follows:

I can never be like his real dad. Harry talks about him all the time. Even Sandy brings him up a lot – he must have been one hell of a guy. It's always the good ones that die. How can I ever hope to measure up to him?
Iain

When I try to be their (step-children's) friend, Ruth says that's not appropriate. When I want to discipline them, she gets hot under the collar. If I just ignore their bad behaviour, she says that I leave all the tough stuff to her – how can I win? I feel like a real flop!
Stephen

I know they don't love me ... and I don't even expect them to. I want them to like me, though. But whatever I do doesn't seem to make any difference. It feels like I am losing out on all counts. Even Rachel (partner) thinks that I'm not trying hard enough. So, where do I go from here?

John

Embarrassed and ashamed of admitting what we consider to be our failure as step-parents, we often struggle on our own – isolated, lonely and desperate. It is very important to understand that many other step-parents fight the same battles and feel the same way. We need to shake off the mantle of shame, take courage and move out of our place of loneliness and isolation.

Feelings of inadequacy, loneliness, shame and failure are common to people in the step-parenting role. It is also common to feel confused and resentful, anxious and wicked, cheated and rejected, overwhelmed and despairing. Understanding this came as an enormous relief to me, as I had spent years living with the belief that it was 'just me' and had been painfully aware that carrying this belief had done nothing towards making the situation easier or more bearable. In fact, it had created more problems by producing a giant burden of guilt, which added even more weight to my already heavy load.

As a step-parent it is essential to your emotional well-being to find a good support mechanism. Keep your old friendships well and alive, but remember that only those in step-parenting roles are likely to comprehend your predicament. While there may be exceptions, your childless friends are unlikely to understand. Those friends with offspring of their own usually find it difficult to imagine why you are not as besotted with your darlings as they are with theirs. Consulting with any of these people, even if they have been friends for years, may leave you with an even greater sense of failure and isolation. Connecting with other step-parents can be an invaluable step at this point. It is particularly helpful to find someone whose situation is similar to yours; that is, instant mother, stepfather of young children, stepmother of teenagers etc. The more similar your situation, the easier it is for you to empathise with each other. It won't take long to realise that many of the 'unacceptable' and painful feelings you are experiencing are also your newfound friend's constant companions. This recognition will help you understand that your feelings are not terrible, unacceptable and an indication that you are an awful person, but are normal and common to step-parenting. Whilst finding new friends in similar circumstances will be extremely helpful, participating in a step-parenting education program and joining a stepfamily support group will also help you to realise that there are scores of others with the same issues, struggles, hopes and fears. The emergence of such groups is one of the positive aspects of the increase in step- and blended families in recent decades. They also provide a great opportunity to find and make new friends. Even if you don't have much money to spare, participation in one of these groups can be the best investment you are ever likely to make – in fact, it can be the lifesaver of your marriage!

HINTS

- Find a stepfamily education program.
- Join a stepfamily support group.
- Read available information on stepfamilies.
- Create and nurture friendships with other couples in a similar situation.
- Share your feelings with your partner.
- Share your feelings with your new stepfamily friends.
- Support each other in emotional as well as practical ways.

★ **Attention Deficit Hyperactivity Disorder (ADHD)** is thought to be a neurologically based, chronic disorder characterised by such symptoms as distractibility and inattention, lack of short-term memory, impulsivity and hyperactivity. Children who are afflicted with this disorder usually experience significant emotional, social and family problems. ADHD can affect children to varying degrees of severity, with some children literally 'bouncing off the walls' 24 hours a day, seven days a week. In most cases, ADHD creates learning difficulties and causes inappropriate behaviour and difficulty in establishing and keeping friendships. Children with ADHD often suffer permanent frustration and a deep-rooted lack of self-esteem. They frequently feel inadequate, bad or stupid and, unable to either express or escape their torturous internal experiences, they act it out in aggressive, unpredictable and sometimes violent behaviour. Although they hunger for love and affection, their behaviour can be such that it alienates them from friends, society, and even their own families.

ANGER

Failing to achieve my picture-book image of a happy family, I became increasingly resentful of the children whom I saw as the cause of this. I deeply empathised with the 'wicked stepmother' in the story of Hansel and Gretel, convinced that life without my stepchildren would be all that I desired. I was angry with the children's mother (my predicament was her fault after all); angry with their father, who was able to escape to his office every day, leaving me to care for the boys, one of whom continued to be a bundle of misery; angry with the boys for creating such chaos and conflict in my life; and most of all I was furious with myself.

Anger is a common emotion experienced by step-parents, and can be caused by any one of a thousand things. We often find ourselves seething at the children's absent biological parent. The immaturity, hostility or unreliability on the part of the absent biological parent can be the cause of much frustration and anger in matters of visitation, finance and discipline, as well as in many other areas.

Children are sometimes used in a former partner's attempts to manipulate or 'get at' the other parent or the new step-parent. Aside from being harmful to the children, this can create a sense of helpless fury for the step-parent. Those who feel 'left out', unappreciated and/or unsupported by their partners may experience feelings of resentment and anger, as may those step-parents who feel ignored, rejected or treated with disrespect by their stepchildren. They might also feel angry with themselves for getting into this kind of predicament.

It was difficult for me to acknowledge my anger (even to myself). Having grown up in an environment where anger was never discussed, was usually suppressed and never displayed in a healthy way, I wasn't even sure how to recognise it. Unable to see it for what it was, the anger seemed to 'leak' through every pore of my body. This very quickly began to contaminate almost every aspect of my life. It wasn't long before I found that I was unable to enjoy any one of my relationships — an ominous cloud of unacknowledged and unexpressed anger hanging over them all.

Whatever the cause, it is important to recognise that anger is not a bad or unacceptable emotion, but a warning signal indicating that something in our internal household is not as it should be. Legitimate anger, which is the anger that we feel in response to someone hurting us, can be a useful motivator to do something about the situation. Inappropriate anger,

which is anger that arises without legitimate provocation, is always an over-reaction to an event. It tells us that we need to look behind the scenes to find out what's going on. Anger may be the blanket we use to cover our feelings of failure, our insecurities, guilt and sense of helplessness. Most often we are not consciously aware of these layers of emotion hidden by the mask of anger. In order to 'survive' our step-parenting experience, it is important to look behind the obvious. Much precious emotional energy can be wasted on feeling angry, when the area in which our energy should be expended is in finding ways to overcome our sense of failure.

Another important step that helps to harness our energy is learning to express anger appropriately. This is often easier said than done, as many of us have been raised with the belief that anger is a bad or unacceptable emotion, whilst others (usually those whose caregivers' anger had been out of control) are terrified of any signs of anger. Yet others let loose tirades of rage they consider to be 'their right and privilege', not realising or simply not caring about the damage they cause to those around them. If we do not have an awareness of these dynamics we may find ourselves faced with feelings of chaos, confusion and guilt that can result from an unexpected angry outburst or from those volcanic feelings we hide inside. The following questions provide important clues about how you handle your anger.

In response to something that offends you, infuriates you or you do not like:

- Do you seethe inwardly but smile on the outside?
- Do you tell yourself that you have no right to feel this way?
- Do you scream and rage at anyone unfortunate enough to be near you?
- Do you become 'cold' towards the offending person?
- Do you smile at the person who caused your anger and then get back at them in some other way?
- Do you feel guilty for feeling angry?
- Do you worry about losing control?
- Do you have feelings that you want to express in violence?
- Do you drown your anger in alcohol, stuff it down with food or escape it through drugs?
- Do you never get angry at all?
- Do you displace your anger? For example, do you find

yourself screaming at the kids or kicking the cat after encountering the 'ex' (when you felt you couldn't say what you wanted)?

If you answered 'yes' to any of these questions, you can enhance your own emotional health and the success of your stepfamily relationships by embracing different ways of dealing with your angry feelings.

The first step is to be honest about your feelings. When you are angry, acknowledge and 'own' your anger. Even if you are angry because the 'ex' has changed the visiting arrangements for the third time, your partner is off on a golfing weekend and you are 'stranded' with his darlings, or the 'wretched' kid is having a screaming fit, accept the anger as your own – in other words, don't blame it on the 'offender'. By the same token, it is unhelpful to repress this anger by pretending that these things leave you cool as a cucumber. After acknowledging that you are angry, **the second step** is to consider the thoughts that accompany your emotion. You might even like to write them down so you can examine them more carefully later (when you have cooled down). If you think, for instance, that you are being treated like a housekeeper by your partner, who has left you to take care of the children whilst enjoying himself on the golf course, chances are that underneath your anger is a layer of hurt – possibly made up of what you consider to be your partner's selfishness, his lack of consideration for you and your needs and his expectation that you will take care of things. Recognising this for what it is will stand you in good stead when you take **the third step**, which is confronting the issue by raising it with your partner. Rather than blowing up and spilling out your resentment, frustration and anger, explain clearly how his actions caused you to feel. Addressing the difficulty in this way has a number of benefits: rather than putting your partner into an immediate position of defence, which is the position most people take when they feel attacked, it allows him to remain sufficiently open to hear what you have to say. It helps him see the situation from your point of view, which might be an absolute revelation to him. It is likely that he did not think about his weekend away in those terms and that he certainly did not intend to hurt you. It gives him an opportunity to apologise. Whatever his response, it is always useful to discover the real emotions that may be hiding under the cover of anger, if for no other reason than for the purpose of growing in your own awareness.

Over time I came to realise that not all of my anger was connected to my current situation. Some of my anger belonged in my past. This discovery helped me to explore my anger in its original context and to release it more appropriately. After I gained some practice in this I found that things didn't 'rattle' me anywhere near as much as they had done previously. Life became much more peaceful as a consequence!

Remember that anger is a normal emotion. It is not unique to you and it is no indication that your feelings are wrong, bad or unacceptable. The most important issue relating to anger is how you handle it. While it is a normal emotion that should neither be rationalised nor denied, do not allow your anger to control you. Anger that controls can turn into uncontrollable anger. Uncontrollable anger is dangerous – it hurts others and it hurts you. Uncontrollable anger or rage damages people, relationships and you – **if you experience this kind of anger or rage, professional help is 'a must'**!

Take responsibility for your anger. Recognise that it is your response to a stimulus. No one outside yourself can force you to feel anything, not even anger! Talking through your anger with the offending person or talking about the issue with a good listener may help. Getting rid of the anger energy is always advisable. This could be achieved by going for a run, scrubbing the kitchen floor or vigorously digging the garden. If you find that your anger was inappropriate, don't send yourself on a guilt trip. Instead, say 'sorry'. If you had good reason for it, sort it out and let it go!

HINTS

- Acknowledge your anger. Remember, it is a normal human emotion.
- Take responsibility for and 'own' your anger.
- Explore your angry thoughts.
- Find out where your anger really belongs.

- Explore the emotions that might be hiding underneath your angry mask.
- Don't allow the anger to control you.
- Talk it out and resolve the issue.
- Talk it over and find an appropriate course of action.
- Get rid of the anger energy.
- Don't go on a guilt trip.
- Let go!

Remember, if you experience uncontrollable anger, seek professional help!

IT'S ALL MY
FAULT!

A close companion to my feelings of failure and my bouts of anger were my feelings of guilt. I felt guilty because I never seemed to be able to live up to the expectations I had of myself (which I didn't know at the time were mostly unrealistic). I felt guilt for my inability to create what I pictured to be a harmonious home; for the resentment I often felt of my stepsons; for yearning for my uncomplicated, single, 'pre-kids' life; for wanting my husband and all his attention for myself; for wishing to 'return the kids to sender'; for wanting to run away … the list was endless. Most of all, however, I felt guilty for not being the mother of my dreams — supermum.

In time I came to understand that guilt is one of the major painful emotions experienced in stepfamilies. The causes may be many and varied, but are often related to the way step-parents feel about their stepchildren. Feelings shared with me in my counselling role range from mild resentment and irritation to hatred and rage.

Stepchildren are sometimes regarded as a major intrusion in the step-parent's life. Childless step-parents of younger children frequently are ill-prepared for the time, effort and energy required by their charges. They can find themselves reeling under the burden they had not anticipated, but may at the same time have committed to 'stick it out' despite their difficulties. I have found this type of step-parent to be particularly prone to feelings of guilt, often torn by the desire to create a happy home and the urge to run away from home. Step-parents who have children of their own may feel guilt over issues of discipline and fairness. This can be an even bigger problem if they dislike their partner's children and lean towards preferential treatment of their own. Step-parents may feel guilt over many issues including financial matters, custodial or access disputes, ex-spouse complaints etc.

Step-parents may have feelings of guilt if they were instrumental (or perceived to be instrumental) in their new partner's marriage break-up, if they are unable to 'win over' their stepchildren, if their new partner displays disinterest in his or her biological children or is unwilling to take the appropriate level of responsibility for them. Step-parents might feel guilty if the children's biological parent is too resentful to allow the former partner reasonable access to the children, if the partner shows more interest in their stepchildren than their biological offspring, if the children are being manipulated or are used as pawns in a wrangle between disputing adults, and so on.

Some of the reasons stepmothers have shared with me for their feelings of guilt are:

- I don't like his kids.
- I am jealous of the time he spends with them.
- I was the reason he left his family, and I can see now how much it has hurt them.
- His children aren't happy when they come to see us.
- I can't be a good mother to his children.
- His children don't like me.
- I have no control over what happens to them at their biological mother's house, and she's totally irresponsible.
- He relates better to my kids than to his own.
- The kids have huge emotional problems.
- I raised them and they didn't turn out right.
- I needed more space for me and my kids. I tried to hide my resentment but it leaked out anyway.

Stepfathers share their guilty thoughts:

- Most of the money goes to my 'ex' and there just doesn't seem to be enough for all of us.
- I know I let my children get away with murder, but I see them so rarely, what else am I supposed to do?
- My ex-wife can't cope with the kids, but my new partner doesn't want them living with us either.
- I just don't have enough time to spend with anyone, not my kids, not my step-kids, not even with my wife – so no one's happy and I feel like I'm constantly being torn in all directions.

- I can't stand her boys, they look like her 'ex' and they are just as obnoxious.
- The kids are so rotten to Sandra (new partner) but nothing I do seems to make any difference.

Although, as the examples show, stepfathers are not exempt from feelings of guilt, it seems that stepmothers are more adept at 'perfecting the art'. Could this be the result of how we have been portrayed throughout history? Fairytale images of wicked stepmothers, perpetuated through literature, film and other media have certainly not done much for our self-esteem, and neither have images of the 'perfect', ever-patient, kind and loving stepmother who comes to the rescue of the handsome (but domestically challenged) father, left to fend for himself after the death of his wife. Even the modern Hollywood version of the stepmother (Julia Roberts in 'Stepmom') abandons a successful career as a fashion photographer to care for her stepchildren. No wonder we are in trouble, if these are our role models. It takes a very self-confident and mature person to find her own balance. Attempting to 'live down' the wicked image or to 'live up' to the unrealistic one is a sure path to failure and, you guessed, it – more guilt!

The Issue of Guilt

Guilt is a complex subject, and there are differing views on where and how it originates, why we experience it, whether it is useful or destructive and so on. For the purposes of this book, I have chosen to examine the issue of guilt by looking at it as an appropriate or inappropriate response. As seen from this perspective, appropriate guilt is the emotion we feel when we do something that does not agree with the standards on which we have built our lives. As such it can propel us into the kind of action that will help us change whatever we identify as the cause of our guilt. In this case, guilt can be regarded as useful. The other kind of guilt is usually based on faulty thinking and is the result of unrealistic expectations. In such cases, guilt can become a barrier to positive change.

Our standards normally are a reflection of the values absorbed in our childhood years. For instance, if we learn to be honest, respectful, discerning and self-reliant, we gain values that will stand us in good stead in our adult life. However, if our childhood experience is one of abuse, or where we learn that lying avoids pain, pretending brings rewards and rules are never to be questioned, we will eventually be controlled by uncertainty, confusion and pain. The standards we develop if we are parented in a critical, devaluing or manipulative way are often unrealistic and unattainable. If we grow up in an environment in which we feel loved only when we do as we are told, we are likely to develop the belief that nothing short of perfection is good enough and that we must perform in an expected way in order to be valued and loved. This can set us on a path of self-rejection, self-hatred and feeling 'less' than everyone else. We might continually struggle for this kind of perfection, yet feel that we never quite manage to measure up. The critical voice in our heads might scream at us: 'You idiot, why can't you ever get anything right?'; 'this just isn't good enough – if I were like Mary, Jason or Kim, I'd be able to do this properly', the implication being that I **should** do it better. Therefore, it is important that we take a closer look at our standards.

When we feel guilt the suggestion (in our mind) is that we did something wrong – that we are at fault. For instance, if we used our stepchildren as pawns in a game of control and manipulation, if we took advantage of their vulnerability, disrespected their rights, disregarded their needs, devalued their personhood or committed some other kind of offence, then indeed we should feel guilty. If, however, we generally strive to be the best step-parent we are capable of being, then our guilt would be inappropriate. We need to accept that we may fall short of our good intentions, that sometimes the best we have to give may not be good enough and our struggles to 'win them over', are proving to be futile.

Some of the 'shoulds' I have come across in counselling stepmothers are:

- I should love my partner's children.
- I should be a perfect mother/father and wife/ husband/ partner.
- I should not feel resentment, anger, disappointment, confusion, fear, jealousy.
- I should always be patient, kind, loving, caring, generous, accepting, sacrificing.
- I should never be tired, sick, crabby, uncooperative, moody.

- I should always understand my partner, his or her children, the position of the 'ex'.
- I should always give and not expect to take.
- I should be wonder woman and supermum all rolled into one.

Don't think it's just you – everyone has a collection of 'shoulds'! Rather than worrying about it, just examine your 'shoulds' carefully.

Are my standards realistic?
Is it realistic to expect to love my partner's children? (Isn't love something that develops over time? For how long have I known them? Do they behave in a lovable fashion?)

How many perfect mothers/fathers, husbands/wives do I know? (Do they really exist? What does perfect mean anyhow?)

Why shouldn't I feel resentment, anger, disappointment...? (Do I expect that I can just turn my feeling switch to an 'off' position whenever I please? Has this worked for me in other areas of my life? When? Where?)

Are these standards my own, or do they belong to someone else (perhaps my parents or another influential person in my life)?
Who said I should always be loving, patient, kind? (Whose voice do I hear when I think these thoughts – my own or someone else's?)

Whose expectation is it that I should always be generous, accepting and sacrificing? (Is that the way I want to be? What happens if I am not?)

DO I WANT TO RETAIN THESE STANDARDS?

How useful are they? (Do they help me live an authentic life? Do they help or hinder my personal development and growth?)

What effect do they have on the people around me? (Do they help me 'give' freely or 'force' me to do it grudgingly, resenting every step of the way?)

Some of the answers you discover can come as quite a surprise. You may realise that many of the standards you have been struggling to uphold have little to do with the REAL you. Those you discover to be unrealistic, that aren't your standards or that you just don't want any more, need to be dealt with. Whilst this can be quite a difficult task that may require professional assistance, you can certainly give it a good try on your own or, better still, with the help of a trusted friend.

Unrealistic standards once recognised can be replaced with more realistic ones.

Instead of telling yourself that you should love your partner's children, and feeling guilty over actually hating their guts, it is much more useful to say: 'I can't really expect to love my stepkids, especially when I hardly know them. Perhaps I'll grow to love them one day, but right now even just liking them will be a great achievement. So, what needs to happen (what can I do) that might help me like them a bit better?'

'There is no such thing as a perfect mother/father or anyone. As striving towards perfection will always leave me feeling like a failure, it's a much better idea to settle for just doing the best I can and reminding myself that that's all anyone can do.'

Standards that are no more than unexamined souvenirs from your past can either be tossed out or reframed to suit your adult personality.
You'd best begin by tossing out the words 'always' and 'never', as they do little more than create unnecessary pressure. Once you're rid of these, try a reframe:

'I'd like to be patient and kind, loving, caring ... I know I don't always succeed, but then – who does?'

'I enjoy being generous, but it's my choice when and where I express my generosity.'

'Acceptance is a useful quality and I can see its benefit. Sometimes, though, I find it too hard.'

'I'm not sure where the 'sacrificial bit' comes from, but I know for certain that it isn't me. It rather sounds like being a victim and there is no way I'm going to identify with that.'

YOU CAN CHOOSE THE STANDARDS BY WHICH YOU WANT TO LIVE

Understand that you didn't have that choice when you were a child, but now you do and you can exercise it every step of the way.

Any 'I should' that cannot be replaced with words such as 'I choose to', 'I want to', 'I prefer to' or 'I am willing to try' does not serve you well and therefore is best eliminated from your vocabulary.

Armed with this kind of insight and a healthy dose of determination you will find in due time that:

- You can see your situation more clearly.
- You are much freer in the way you respond to others' wishes and requests.
- You can deal far more effectively with any guilt issues in your life that do have substance.

Why do I Feel Guilty?

The step-parenting experience is fertile breeding ground for both appropriate and inappropriate guilt. Therefore, it is important to examine the reason/s that cause you to feel this way. If you have done something that has violated a standard you regard as useful and important in your adult life, the best way to deal with this is to 'own up'. Depending on the situation, you may need to acknowledge your fault to the person who was the recipient of your inappropriate action. Sometimes 'owning up' to yourself is enough. Admitting your faults and failings to yourself is always the first step in the right direction, as you can only change that which you acknowledge. This is illustrated by Sam:

After every access visit I felt bad. I knew it wasn't fair, but every time I saw her boys, I'd get really depressed. It'd be like Beth changed personality or something. I was no longer important and the kids couldn't do anything wrong. Even after they left she'd carry on and on about her 'precious boys' – how they were the greatest, smartest – the best. How could I compete with that? I used to treat them okay, but I knew that they could sense my hostility. It was obvious I had to do something about that – after all, it wasn't their fault.

Once Sam recognised that he was struggling with feelings of jealousy, he was able to make appropriate changes. Acknowledging his feelings (just to himself) soon helped him treat his stepsons with more genuine kindness, which rapidly relieved him of his guilt.

Sometimes 'owning up' to ourselves is not enough, and an apology and/or some recompensive action are in order, as Karen discovered:

I knew that I was treating them unequally. Although his daughter was the same age as mine, I just couldn't let her do the same things. She wasn't as mature and reliable, and couldn't be trusted. I did feel pretty mean, but thought I was right. It was only when my daughter, who had gotten along quite well with her stepsister, started treating her like a 'nitwit', it dawned on me that the way I treated her had something to do with that. I really felt guilty then.

Karen was only able to allay her guilt by apologising to both her stepdaughter and her daughter for the unequal treatment that she had justified in her own mind. Once she realised how unreasonable and unhelpful her behaviour had been, she was also able to adjust the way she dealt with the children.

It's All My Fault

If you carry with you a constant sense of guilt, if your 'should' basket is filled to overflowing or if you cannot shake the uncomfortable feeling that if it wasn't for you everything would be better (the family would thrive, your partner would be happier, your stepchildren would be perfect little angels, the world would be a better place), then you should consider seeking the help of a professional (see pages 163-7).

Whatever the reason for your guilty feelings, you can be sure that they are only useful if they stir you into appropriate action. Indulging in feelings of guilt for any length of time is neither useful nor healthy. Guilt can make you sick, anxious and depressed if you choose not to deal with it. Guilt, whether appropriate or inappropriate, requires forgiveness. It is important that you learn to forgive yourself for those real or perceived failures that caused the guilt in the first place.

HINTS

Identify your guilt and decide whether it is appropriate or inappropriate.

In the case of appropriate guilt:

- Own up – take responsibility for your actions.
- Make up – say 'I am sorry', make good your mistake, make recompense.
- Forgive yourself and let go of the guilt feeling!

In the case of inappropriate guilt:

Ask yourself:

- What did I do wrong?
- Is the situation that is causing my guilt out of my control?
- Whose standards or expectations am I trying to live up to?
- Do they come from my 'should' basket?
- Do I want to retain these standards?
- What positive outcome can I expect as a result of feeling guilty?

If you feel that you are to blame for most things that go wrong in your life, seek professional assistance.

DADS ARE PEOPLE, TOO

The rising number of divorces and the more recent trend of women preferring to raise offspring on their own means that there is a multitude of fathers who live apart from their children. This may not present a problem for some men, but others experience it as heart-wrenching tragedy. In recent times we have been increasingly confronted with the reality of pain, anguish and distress of fathers who lose fathering rights of their children. Within a system that generally favours custodial rights of mothers, it can be difficult for fathers who wish to take on the role of main caregiver to their children, or those who consider themselves to be better able to raise them than their children's mother, to achieve their aim. The disappointment, sense of injustice and anguish these fathers may experience as a consequence can lead to great desperation that sometimes even ends in tragedy.

Men who are experiencing a deep sense of loss, who are

filled with great resentment and bitterness toward their ex-partners and who feel that they cannot exist on their own may be inclined to step into a ready-made family situation long before they are emotionally ready to do so. Reeling from loss, raw from grief, agonised by the separation from their children, they may operate in the belief that the new family will compensate. This, however, only sets them up for more confusion, greater disappointment and additional pain.

Non-Custodial Fathers/Stepfathers

The decision to separate is rarely made lightly, and usually leaves great pain in its wake. Shock, anger, feelings of failure and guilt may be the initial response. Coming to terms with its finality is often the next difficult step. For the man who, through divorce or separation, loses not only his partner but also his children, a loss of personal identity is almost inevitable. His willingness to accept responsibility for the part he played in the relationship breakdown and how he chooses to move on with his life will largely determine whether and how quickly he regains his sense of self. Some men find the experience so devastating that the only way they feel able to deal with it is to withdraw totally from their family. These men may see a complete break-away as their best option, and may feel that their children would be better off without them. Others may be keen to continue their parenting involvement, but find themselves hindered every step of the way by an unforgiving, hostile former partner. Other men may come to a workable co-parenting agreement with their 'ex'.

The man who rushes into a new relationship to ease his pain of loss (even if he is not consciously aware of this motive) will most likely find himself in deep water. Instead of finding joy in step-parenting his new partner's children, he may encounter intensified feelings of loss and experience painful pangs of guilt. 'It is unfair' his mind may be screaming, 'all this time, effort and love should go to my children'. He may find himself uncomfortably caught between the 'old' and the 'new', with guilt as his constant companion. He may feel guilt about the loss of his first family, even if the separation was not instigated by him. He might feel guilt about the furious rage he may have toward his former partner; about the little time he is able to spend with his biological children; about child support payments that strangle him financially but which his 'ex' complains aren't enough. As Toby explains sadly, 'If I'd known how it would turn out, I would never have agreed to the separation'.

At the same time, the non-custodial stepfather may experience feelings of guilt about not being fully available emotionally to his new family, about spending too much or too little time with his stepchildren or about now having to support his former family financially, which leaves a noticeable dent in the finances he has available to support his new family. Eric complains: 'The kid comes over wearing all this fancy gear and all she (the 'ex') does is whinge about not getting enough of my money'. He may feel guilt about the many different ways his first family intrude upon his new family life. Since he knows this is bitterly resented by his new partner, it leaves him feeling like he's in a 'no-win' situation.

No matter what he does, it seems he is trapped. He is reeling from a multitude of complex problems, when all he really wants to do is get on with his life.

An additional problem may arise for the man whose former spouse takes a new partner. Now another male enters the picture, with whom he may feel the need to compete. Even for the man who wants nothing but the best for his children, it can be like a stab in his heart if his children show signs of liking their stepfather. Jealousy may sear him. He may not be able to bear the thought of being supplanted, and may be gripped by the fear of losing his children to another. As Carl reports with bitterness: 'I feel like punching him out! Whatever I give to Ben (his son), he'll always find something better. Every time I get to see him, he shows me all his new stuff. I think it's really low how this jerk (his stepfather) bribes the kid!'

Men caught in such emotional turmoil are not in a good position to create new beginnings. They short-change their biological children, their new families and, ultimately, themselves. It is of vital importance that they sort through and deal with their hurt and grief before contemplating another relationship, especially one that promises an instant family.

Previously Single Stepfathers

For the previously single man, an instant family life can be fraught with unexpected complications. Having had to care for no-one but himself until now, he may be ill-prepared for this new experience, and his idea of family life could be quite unrealistic. He may be horrified to discover that the children, who barely featured in his plans for the future, are an ever-present reality. They constantly interrupt conversations, disturb sleep, disrupt plans, demand attention and interfere with any notions of romance. They are not only a persistent presence, but also a painful reminder of his partner's past. He may find himself frustrated, perhaps furious with the children for taking up so much of his partner's time and energy. Watching her mothering them may leave him feeling jealous, wondering whether her love for them could be stronger than the love she has for him. Especially in early times of conflict, still insecure in his position, he might feel rebuffed, rejected, left out – viewing his partner and her children as a separate unit with no room for him. His efforts to fit in may feel futile and humiliating.

The children may view his move to take his place at their

mother's side with suspicion, may meet his attempts at parenting with resentment, and his tentative forays into discipline with open hostility. Incurring the children's wrath is also likely to upset their mother, who at this point may be seriously questioning her choice of partner. What the man may consider as finding his role in his newly acquired family might be seen by his partner and her children as unwanted interference and even violation. For him it may feel as though no matter what he does, he cannot win. Faced with such complexities, and coming from the relatively uncomplicated single existence, it is no wonder that men who enter instant family life with few realistic expectations often fail to navigate these difficulties and give up.

The children's access visits with their biological father are often welcomed by the previously single stepfather, as they ensure cherished time alone with their partner. This can provide such a sense of relief, that some men might be tempted to suggest it as a permanent arrangement. This suggestion may not be welcomed by their partner, and could endanger their relationship.

While some men are genuinely pleased about their stepchildren's continuing relationship with their biological father, others might feel threatened by it. Insecure about their own role in the lives of their stepchildren, they may regard the father–child relationship as undermining their own position. They may feel an urge to compete, perhaps a need to prove that they are more responsible, better carers, better providers, better fathers. This rarely achieves the desired result, and places the children in the painful position of feeling they must make a choice between their 'real' dad and their stepfather.

In situations where the biological father is deceased, stepfathers face different challenges. Whilst they don't have to contend with a real-life daddy who knows how to show the kids a good time, they often feel like they have to compete with a bigger than real-life dad, a glorified memory of an image they can never live up to, regardless of how hard they try.

No matter what the situation, an attempt at living up to, making up for, or replacing the children's biological father is always a futile effort destined to fail. Men who find themselves caught in this trap would do well to get out of it as quickly as possible. They and their families are much better served if they expend their energy on building a solid relationship with their new partner. This is the only foundation from which the stepfather can begin to build a good relationship with her children. Once he takes the pressure off himself to replace their dad, he is more likely to succeed at being a great stepdad.

Custodial Fathers/Stepfathers

Although custodial fathers would still not be considered the 'norm', there has been a significant increase over the past decade. In such arrangements the obvious advantages are that fathers are able to keep with them the children they love and they do not need to worry about a hostile former partner whisking them away to another state or country, interfering with their visitation rights and/or creating other contact conflict. While having custody of their children saves some fathers much heartache, it can also be the cause of a major headache.

Being the custodial father of young children can present many difficulties. My husband very quickly discovered this when he became only the second male in New South Wales to be awarded sole custody, care and control of his children. The first question he had to tackle was what to do with the children during his work hours. This is a very important question for any single dad. My husband's dilemma was solved when his mother offered to take care of the boys during the day. Where there is no willing or able family member to take on the job, long day-care or the services of a nanny may need to be considered. The downside of this is that it can place great strain on finances, and so for many dads simply is not an option. Despite help from others, single fathers may not be prepared for the enormous commitment required. The realisation that now every spare moment is accounted for may come as a rude shock. The first weeks and months of sole parenting are often a time of great crisis. Men finding themselves in this situation may still be reeling from whatever caused them to take this enormous step. Whatever the cause, the resultant situation is usually accompanied by pain, anguish, uncertainty, loss, grief and frequently by fear. He not only has to deal with his own emotions but is also called upon to help his children deal with theirs. Losing their mother, whether it be a loss due to her death or due to the parents' separation, is always traumatic. Steering his children through this difficult period, whilst experiencing intense suffering himself, can be an almost superhuman task.

A man who finds himself in such a situation might be inclined to commence another relationship more quickly than is advisable. The need to share the physical burden of caring for his children may be one of his reasons; his desire to share the emotional strain may be another. Although understandable, neither of these reasons build the foundation for a successful new relationship. Custodial fathers who move into a relationship for any of these reasons will sometimes, once remarried, lay the entire burden of their children into their new partner's lap, while feeling as though they have lived up to their responsibility. Women who bring to their relationship a need to rescue this 'suffering man' and to save his 'poor children' will quickly feel angry, resentful and used. If his former wife or partner has died, living in the shadow of her memory can place great stress on the new partner. Where the former partner has left her husband and children, the often unspoken expectations of the new relationship can be just as stressful. Being a better wife, a more responsible person, a more competent mother creates the kind of pressure on the stepmother that carries potential disaster for the relationship. This pressure may be less obvious to the woman who brings to the relationship her own child/ren. Well-versed in mothering, she may recognise these expectations as unrealistic, may take little notice of them and may prove them unnecessary as she tucks his children under her competent wing. If she is in a similar predicament, however, looking for the knight on the white horse to rescue her and her young ones from the dire consequences of her recent relationship breakdown, both partners are in for a rude shock, as both are pursuing their own agendas, and neither will have anything of substance to give to the other.

For couples in these situations, the importance of open communication cannot be sufficiently emphasised. Prospective partners need time and space to get to know each other, to discuss their hopes, their dreams, difficulties, frustrations and fears. Although the temptation may be great, rushing into a new relationship rarely works out for the best.

HINTS

Non-custodial fathers/stepfathers

- Accept responsibility for the part you played in the breakdown of your relationship.
- Work through your feelings of guilt, jealousy and/or fear.
- Resist the urge to compete with your child's stepfather/father.
- Give yourself all the time you need to heal from your relationship breakdown before you contemplate stepfamily life.

Previously single stepfathers

- Accept that your stepchildren are an important part of the 'package'.
- Leave the area of discipline to your partner.

- Resist competitive urges.
- Don't stand between your partner and her children.
- Remember that she loves you as much as (just differently to) her children.

Custodial fathers/stepfathers

Find a safe arrangement for the daytime care of your children.
- Seek the support of other men in similar situations.
- Ensure that you have some 'play' time to yourself.
- Deal with your (and your children's) emotional issues – if necessary, enlist professional help.
- Take time to heal before you re-partner!

STEP-RELATIONSHIPS

Successful stepfamily living depends upon the quality of the relationships shared by the members of the stepfamily. It may be useful to consider the different relationships within a stepfamily.

The Couple Relationship

Stepfamily experts agree that for the couple who have embarked upon stepfamily living, strengthening their relationship is the most important task. This easily can be neglected in the couple's eagerness to create a new home and family life for their respective children. It needs to be given top priority, however, since their new family's continuing existence and well-being is directly related to how the couple fare in this department.

A clear commitment to your relationship is a 'must'. Thinking that you can just split up if things don't work out does not make for a solid foundation.

INTIMACY

Intimacy is often the first victim of the step-parenting experience. Children appearing in your bedroom at all hours of the night, little ones demanding your attention before the break of dawn, teenage stepchildren making your night into their day, squabbles and scrapes – every aspect of the exhausting reality of step-parenthood can play havoc with your desire for and feelings of intimacy. Whilst your sex life only represents one aspect of intimacy with your partner, it is usually a rather important one. It may also be the one that suffers most in the initial stage of stepfamily living. All but drowning in the multitude of demands upon your time and energy, lovemaking might be the last thing on your mind. The one with amorous intentions is not usually the one who got up three times throughout the night (to feed the baby, change wet sheets or chase away a child's nightmare).

Some may disagree, but my experience tells me that, although we live in an enlightened age, it is typically the woman who takes care of all these 'little jobs'. It is also the woman who is more inclined to be 'turned off' when feeling cheated, short-changed, ignored or unappreciated, and (dare I say it) the woman who is more inclined to use her sexual availability as a weapon. Although she could defend this as her only means of being 'heard', it is a very unhealthy way of communicating and carries the potential to destroy any chance of achieving the desired state of intimacy. While the man's sexual desire is not normally as readily affected, it can be equally diminished by feelings of worry, anxiety and stress. If the step-parenting experience causes him to live in a

moments of intimacy are rare

constant state of 'angst' it may not be long before your sex life becomes a mere memory and your levels of intimacy are sadly depleted. This is not conducive to the establishment or maintenance of a satisfying couple relationship.

It is important to remember that, whilst lovemaking is a vital expression of intimacy, the state of intimacy entails so much more. Intimacy is the container that holds such treasures as commitment, trust, vulnerability, giving value and worth to your partner, allowing them to be who they are, giving and receiving – in short, an expression of emotional connectedness. As this container is rather fragile (especially at the beginning of a relationship), it needs to be treated as such and should be cherished, protected and nurtured:

- You cherish it when you put the relationship with your partner before all other relationships.
- You protect it when you treat your partner with the same consideration and respect with which you desire to be treated.
- You nurture it when you allow yourself to be open and vulnerable with your partner.

Creating and maintaining intimacy in a stepfamily situation requires as much work as all other aspects of the relationship. Accepting that you will come across hurdles, such as mentioned above, will assist you in not allowing them to wreak havoc with your emotional connection. Being open about your feelings, expectations, disappointments, concerns and fears (rather than exploding or withdrawing) will help you pour your energy into seeking solutions to your dilemmas. It will put you both on the same side of the fence (so to speak), strengthen your emotional connection and increase your level of intimacy.

TIME OUT

As a couple, time away from the children, time spent apart from your daily stresses, worries and concerns, time spent in a shared hobby, relaxation time and time for romancing each other, are essential. If the circumstances are such that it may seem impossible to take time out, it is important to find a solution. You may need to enlist the help of grandparents, friends or babysitters to achieve this goal. If you find asking for help difficult, now is a good time to overcome this difficulty. Build time out together into your day, even if it is only for a 15–20-minute period. Make a weekly appointment with each other. You could spend some time having coffee together, share a walk around the block, go to the movies, have dinner at a restaurant or do any one of a number of things that you both might enjoy. Ensure that you have a full day together on a monthly basis and a holiday alone (without the children) once a year. This holiday can be as long or as short as you can afford and are able to fit into your lifestyle. The important aspect is that it is a childless break and enables you to leave your daily cares behind.

COMMUNICATION

Another important issue in forging a strong couple bond is communication. In order to become artful at this, it is necessary to learn to express your feelings appropriately. This, of course, is a lot easier when your feelings are pleasant and happy ones. When your emotions are those of anger, frustration, resentment or helplessness, however, their expression becomes a much greater challenge. When expressing these, as illustrated in an earlier chapter, it is of particular importance not to blame your partner or his/her children for your feelings. Accepting responsibility for your feelings helps you to keep your communication open and your partner to hear what you are saying, and it makes problem solving a more likely outcome. It paves the way for you to say what you need, want, don't like and don't want. Remember, your partner is not a mind reader. She or he cannot possibly know what thoughts, feelings, wishes or desires you have without you sharing this information. It is equally important that your partner has the opportunity to communicate with you in the same fashion and that you listen as carefully and as non-defensively as you expect from him or her.

CONFLICT

Don't shy away from conflict. It is a natural part of togetherness and, handled wisely, will help you and your partner to become more authentic in your relationship. Authenticity involves the free expression of yourself as you really are. The ability to 'be yourself' (rather than wearing masks) with your partner is one of the most important foundations of a healthy and lasting relationship. So, as long as you remember your commitment to the relationship, that you are in this together for better or for worse, that this conflict is not going to drive you apart, that it is not the end of the road but potentially the beginning of a more functional one, then conflict is an important and healthy process.

A few points that will help you deal with conflict:

- Don't deal with the issue causing conflict in the heat of the moment. Only saints are objective at that time. Do yourself a favour and leave some time between the incident and your discussion.
- Deal with the issue at hand. Dredging up everything that has annoyed you about each other during the past five years is not helpful.

- Don't threaten or manipulate, and don't call each other names. Even if you are dying to let something nasty slip from your lips, you will only regret it later.

- Give each other turns to say what you wish to say. When it is the other's turn, listen carefully and seek to understand what they are saying from their point of view.

- Don't be afraid of discovering that you are wrong. If you are, say 'sorry'!

- If your partner is the one who needs to apologise, be gracious in accepting the apology. It's better to bite your tongue than to say, 'I told you so'!

- The issue causing conflict may not be a matter of right or wrong – you may need to 'agree to disagree'. There are no rules that you must always be of the same opinion. Accepting your partner's differing views, beliefs, thoughts and feelings attests to a healthy relationship.

- 'Meeting halfway' may be a necessary compromise to achieving the resolution of your conflict. This becomes much easier if you remember that partnerships require a lot of 'give and take' in order to be successful.

- Don't let the sun go down without at least being on the way toward a resolution. Some people say that 'making up' is the best part of conflict. Why not give it a try?

- Celebrate the successful resolution of your conflict!

SUPPORT

It is a most important aspect of the couple relationship that you stand united before the children. In dealing with them, it is absolutely essential that you support each other.

Children, especially in stepfamily situations, sometimes attempt to divide and conquer. Nothing has quite the same potential to cause a step-parent to feel left out, useless and helpless as when their partner sides with his/her children. This, more than any other difficulty one might encounter, has the power to annihilate the couple relationship. Feelings of guilt, over-protectiveness, the desire to make things up to the children, fear of their partner acting unfairly, or a number of other reasons cause almost all biological parents in a stepfamily situation to fall into this trap at least once. Whilst understandable, this must be guarded against at all costs. Such a situation not only questions the position of the new step-parent but also diminishes their authority in the eyes of the children. If either of you have overstepped your mark, this certainly needs to be discussed and worked out – but it should be done away from the children's eyes and ears. In order to avoid such situations, it is important to be clear on the expectations you each have of the children, and to ensure they are realistic and well defined. It also helps to remember that the expectations of children need to be kept age-appropriate and, at least in the early days of the new family's formation, should be few and flexible. Standing united in this matter helps the step-parent feel valued and respected, and gives the children feelings of stability and security.

HINTS

Remember the keys to strengthening your relationship:

1. Invest time, energy and effort to create true intimacy with your partner.
2. Make time spent with your partner a top priority.
3. Practise effective communication skills.
4. Welcome conflict and handle it wisely.
5. Support each other and show your collective children that you are a united front.

Relationship with Stepchildren

Developing a good relationship with your stepchildren can be easier than you expect or a lot harder than you had anticipated. This may have to do with the children's ages and stages in life, it may have to do with their personalities or be simply a matter of liking or disliking each other. The way they relate to you often also depends on the influence of their biological mother. If their mother 'hates your guts', it will most likely affect how her children feel about you. Sometimes children who greeted your intended marriage with enthusiasm turn against you once you have actually 'tied the knot'. Whatever the case may be, when you married you got a package deal. Whether you like it or not, it is now up to you to make the best of it.

Not expecting to feel instant love for the children or to have their instant affection will go a long way towards making the first few months of your stepfamily journey more successful. All new relationships take time to develop, so remember that time is on your side. Help this process along by showing an interest in the things that interest your stepchildren. Spending time together without your partner, perhaps doing something fun together, assists in getting to know each other. This is one area in which dealing with younger stepchildren is a definite advantage, as they are usually less resistant to allowing you into their lives.

Teenage stepchildren can pose a particular challenge. When sharing your new household with a teenager, it is helpful to remember that even biological parents can be in deep despair over their adolescent's antics, and frequently find themselves ill-equipped to effectively deal with them. Expecting teenagers to happily join the family outing you have carefully planned as a special bonding experience is an expectation doomed to failure. Teenagers, whose developmental task is the separation from parents, are not likely to be overjoyed by your attempts to draw them into the new family circle. Creating a relationship with your adolescent stepchildren requires much trial and error, patience, cunning and elephant skin. You may find that your adolescent stepchild (in much the same way as most biological teenagers) responds more favourably to you making use of opportunities for connecting with them that arise spontaneously, rather than attempting to create opportunities that could feel artificial. You can count yourself lucky if you are able to talk them into a shopping trip or some other shared experience. This is much more likely to happen if you come up with something they are absolutely desperate to do and cannot do in the absence of an adult. Your partner's understanding and willingness to step into the background on such occasions is very helpful. Your partner's support, which is crucial in dealing with a stepchild of any age, is absolutely essential in dealing with the adolescent stepchild.

DISCIPLINE

There is general agreement among professionals that, at least in the beginning months and sometimes in the first year or two of the stepfamily journey, disciplining the child should be the task of the biological parent. Children do not take kindly to being told what to do, how to behave etc. by an almost perfect stranger. No doubt many a step-parent has been the recipient of a child's angry outburst: 'You can't tell me what to do, you are not my mother/father!' Punishing children for such outbursts is never helpful. Any disciplinary measures need to be agreed between you and your partner. They should take into consideration the child's age and be firm but flexible. Essentially, both you and your partner should be comfortable with the chosen method. The danger of harsh disciplining or violence has been identified as being greater in the step-parenting arena than in a biological parenting situation. Violence of any type is an unacceptable means of punishment. Violence inflicted or threatened by a stepchild obviously counts as equally unacceptable. If you find yourself unsure of how to deal with disciplinary issues in your home, reading good parenting material and/or attending well-regarded parenting courses can set you on the right path. Especially if you are not too fond of your stepchildren, fairness, even if it seems impossible, is all-important to the development of a good relationship.

As mentioned previously, providing children with their own space is also considered helpful to the creation of harmonious stepfamily living. Whilst having their own room is ideal, if this is impossible give them a nook or cranny for themselves − a special drawer filled with their treasures, a toy box, a wardrobe that is off-limits to other inhabitants of your home − in short, something they can call their own.

HINTS

- Don't expect instant love for or from your stepchildren.
- Show interest in the things that are of interest to them.
- Spend time with them.
- Let your partner take care of disciplining your stepchildren.
- Acquire parenting skills.
- Create some space in your home that belongs to them.

Relationship with Biological Children

Moving into stepfamily living means change for all concerned. Change can be a very threatening prospect, especially to those who have little say in the matter. This is how it may feel for your biological children. Although you might be ready to move on with your life, they may still be actively grieving for the losses experienced as a result of your relationship break-up. They might be lost in their favourite fantasy in which you and their other biological parent rejoin and live 'happily every after'. Then again, they might like the situation as it is, without the other parent. Their life might have taken on a new meaning when they became the 'little man' or 'little woman' of the house – the main focus of your attention, affection and time. In their mind's eye they might see their special relationship with you disappearing. They might fear losing you!

NEEDS

Although anticipating that the move into a new family may be an exciting and all-consuming prospect (for you), it is vitally important to be aware of and sensitive to the feelings of your children. This must also be remembered when you find yourself snowed under by the many demands of your new family. Don't let your eagerness to impress and win over your stepchildren distract you from the needs of your biological children. It is especially at this time that your own children need your attention, your continued affirmation and complete security in the knowledge of your love. This is best achieved by making special time for them. So, as well as telling them how important and precious they are to you, show them by doing some fun things together. Perhaps both you and your partner could incorporate a fortnightly or monthly special date with your respective biological children. It is also important to allow your children to tell you about their unhappiness, discontent and difficulties in adjusting to the new situation. When this happens it is important to remember that this is not about you but about the child. You don't have to defend your decision to marry 'this horrible person' or to allow their 'dreadful children' to live with you etc. When your children entrust you with their feelings, just accept them for what they are, listen to them, empathise with them by saying things like 'yes, I know this is hard for you' and get on with the business of your new life. You may not necessarily change anything about the situation, but your children should feel that you understand. Obviously, if the children's complaints are due to more than adjustment difficulties, you need to investigate and ensure their protection and safety. Always take them seriously if they tell you about physical, emotional or sexual harassment by anyone, even if it implicates their step-parent or a stepsibling. Although this is a terrifying thought, don't think that it can't happen in your home. If it does, it must be dealt with appropriately. Abuse of any kind must never be tolerated! As your children's feelings of safety are largely determined by how readily they can communicate with you, it pays above all else to ensure that the communication channels between you and them remain open.

HINTS

- Be sensitive to the needs of your children.
- Make special time just for them.
- Give them permission to be honest in expressing their thoughts and feelings.
- Ensure you show and tell them OFTEN how much you love them.

Stepsibling Relationships

Stepsiblings may like or loathe each other. They may naturally 'click' and readily form a friendship, cherishing the time they spend together, or they may be wary of the others and merely tolerate them. They could discover an instant dislike, resentment and even hatred for their stepsiblings. This could be due to personality clashes ('I just can't stand them!'), to issues of loyalty ('Why should I like the stupid kid of the horrible person that's stolen my mum/dad?'), jealousy ('They are getting all of my mum's/dad's love') or different beliefs and values ('They lie all the time. How can I be friends with someone like that?') Naturally, stepsibling relationships have a significant impact on the functioning of the family. It is difficult, to say the least, to create happiness in a home that constantly resembles a war zone.

HINTS

- Find out what it is the children dislike about each other.
- Help them to see the situation from the other child's perspective.
- Allow them to talk about their feelings without minimising them.
- Tell them that, whilst you accept their feelings, they still need to make an effort to get along with their stepsiblings.
- Look for compromises that help the family to function more peacefully.
- Be patient – time and increasing familiarity may take care of this issue.
- If you find all this beyond your capability or energy, seek family therapy.

Family Relationships

Family conferences have been found useful by many stepfamilies. The conference could take place once a week, once a fortnight or even once a month (some families find it easier to just let them happen spontaneously), and should be the time when everyone gets to talk about their areas of difficulty. Goals can be set, solutions sought, brainstorming encouraged, chores divided between family members etc. For these meetings to achieve the desired result, everyone needs to feel safe to express their thoughts, feelings, likes, dislikes and concerns. It is the adults' responsibility to create the safety aspect. Rules about how concerns and dislikes are communicated are important. It is equally important to show respect for everyone's input and ideas, regardless of whether the adults or the children agree or disagree with the ideas that are voiced. The children need to be encouraged to express themselves honestly and openly. Family conferences provide a good opportunity for adults to model effective communication skills. Train your collective children to use language that shows that they take responsibility for their feelings. Help them to reframe complaints like 'She makes me so mad when she barges into my room' to 'I get so mad when she barges into my room'. While this is only a small change in the words used, it can make a huge difference in the way this complaint is received. Taking responsibility by saying how **I feel**, rather than suggesting that it's his or her behaviour that is responsible for my feelings, we have a much better chance of being heard by the 'offender'. Family meetings also provide a forum for everyone to voice their needs; for example:

Mum: 'I find it hard when everyone leaves their stuff laying about and the tidy-up work is left to me. For this family to function properly I need everybody's help.'

Dad's child: 'I don't like it when the others (biological children) pick on me. I want them to stop it'.

Dad: 'I am weary when I get home from work. I can't give everyone my attention as soon as I walk through the door – I need 15 minutes to relax before I can be there for you'.

Mum's child: 'I hate it when you use different standards for them (stepchildren). It's unfair and I want the same treatment.'

Allowing your family the freedom to say what they think, feel and need not only helps create trust, but also ensures that family difficulties and annoyances are not overlooked, deemed unimportant or just get 'brushed under the carpet'. Having heard the individual's complaints it is important also to brainstorm and discuss solutions. They could look something like this:

a Make a list of all the things that need to be done. Find out who prefers to do what (Ben mightn't mind vacuuming too much, Lisa might prefer dusting and it might suit Karen to do the washing up). Draw up a schedule of the chores each person agrees to do and state by when they need to be done.

b Find out what 'being picked on' means to the child concerned. Help the other children understand how the child feels about being treated in such a way. Obtain their agreement to stop this behaviour.

c Let the children know that after your 15-minute break you will be able to listen to them, help them, play with them – in short, be available to them. If there are a number of children vying for your attention, it might be important to specify a certain time-frame for each child.

d If there is a good reason to use different standards for your stepchildren and your biological children, explain your reasoning. If there isn't a good reason, find out how they would like things to change and implement the changes.

HINTS

- Hold regular family conferences.
- Model effective communication skills.
- Encourage all stepfamily members (including yourself) to air their views.

Relating with Your Former Partner

This can be a tricky issue, as 'exes' come in all shapes and sizes. If the relationship with your former partner is a good one and you both agree on issues pertaining to your children, the benefits are substantial. If, however, there is acrimony and hostility between the two of you, your children are the ones who suffer the consequences. This makes it very important, regardless of your feelings about your former partner, to display a civil attitude. Naturally, as you have little control over your ex-partner's behaviour, this can be a challenging issue.

Regardless of how each of you feel toward the other, the children must be protected from any battles you may have. They should not be used as go-betweens, spies, carriers of bitterness or tools of manipulation. They should never be the recipient of the wrath you feel towards their other parent, be mistreated because they may look, sound or act like him or her, punished because they would rather be with him or her than with you, despised because they feel an urge to defend and protect their other parent (even if you don't consider him or her to be a good, responsible and deserving parent).

Because children draw their sense of identity from each of their parents, speaking ill of their other parent not only invites an instant defensive response, but may (in their mind) also call into doubt the quality of their own character. It may offend their sense of loyalty and, more than likely, will have an opposite effect to the one you might have intended. Open hostility between biological parents has the potential to tear the child in half. Therefore, it is crucial that you keep whatever axe you may have to grind with your former partner between the two of you. Ideally, children should be allowed to move freely between the two homes and be welcomed and accepted as part of the family in each.

HINTS

- Display a civil attitude towards your 'ex'.
- Keep any negative thoughts about him or her to yourself.
- If unavoidable, fight your battles away from the eyes and ears of your children.
- Never use your children to 'get at' your former partner.

Relating with Your Partner's 'Ex'

This is often a very difficult issue, since their partner's former wife is frequently the one that stepmothers hate with a passion. As Carrie fumes: 'It's her fault that their marriage didn't survive. She's downright crazy and made his life a total misery. She doesn't even look after the kids – they are totally neglected, but she carries on like I am the one who's a bad mother'. Whilst for many second wives or partners their greatest wish is for the 'ex' to disappear from the face of the earth, most are reminded of her existence every time they are faced with her children. When the 'ex' has bad feelings for you, this unfortunately can have a dire effect on your relationship with her children. They may become carriers of her hatred, jealousy or contempt, and report gleefully things she says about you which understandably makes relating to your stepchildren very difficult. In such a situation your partner's support is essential. It will be his job to speak to his children about this and insist that they show respect for you. It will be necessary that he make it clear to his former partner what damage this can cause. His speaking to the 'ex' does not guarantee success, however, and can even serve to inflame the situation. Although the temptation to retaliate in such a circumstance must be great, my strong advice is that you resist this at all costs. Not only would this create even more family unrest, it would have a negative effect on the children, who are caught in the middle of this battle. If you manage to hold out long enough the children will eventually make up their own minds. It is equally unhelpful to compete with the 'ex'. Attempting to prove to your partner that you are a much better spouse and to convince the children that you are a better mother is doomed to failure. Naturally, all of the above may apply also to stepfathers.

It's often their feelings of powerlessness that causes step-parents the greatest grief. Santos reports:

> 'He didn't just leave Myra, he actually abandoned the kids and didn't see them for years. Now that we are together he wants to play the dutiful father. He indoctrinates the kids and they are so damned confused, they don't know whether they are coming or going. It'd be much better if he just took off again and left us all in peace.'

Gabrielle states angrily:

> 'She holds all the cards. When she doesn't like something she just changes access arrangements. She poisons the kids and manipulates us through them. Forget the wicked stepmother, it's the mother that is the wicked one in our case and it makes me so mad, I want to scratch her eyes out'.

Although it is terribly frustrating to deal with an 'ex' like that, it is important that you don't allow your feelings about him or her to influence your response to the children. Hard as it may be, you need to remember that they, like you, are innocent victims in this tragic game. Taking your feelings out on them is unfair and provides no solution to the problem. You may need to come to terms with the possibility that there may be no solution to this problem. In such a situation you can only hope that in time the unreasonable 'ex' will grow tired of playing his or her destructive games and wise up to the damage he or she is causing the children, or that some change in circumstances will create the desired results. I know this is not very satisfying, but it is the unfortunate reality for some.

HINTS

- Resist the urge to compete with your partner's 'ex'.
- Determine that no matter what your partner's 'ex' may do, you won't let it rattle you.

- Don't take out your frustration on his or her children.
- No matter how tempting, do not retaliate!

Relationships with 'In-Laws'

In stepfamily situations it is often the grandparents who draw the shortest straw. Through no fault of their own, merely because they happen to be one of the involved party's parents, they may end up losing their relationship with the grandchildren they cherish and love. Needless to say, this can be a heartbreaking experience for the grandparents as well as the grandchildren concerned. Cutting grandparents out of the children's and/or stepchildren's lives, without a very good reason to do so, does not serve anyone well. Distancing your family from them may be warranted if they are bitter and hostile toward you and attempt to poison the children with their views, thus hindering their successful integration into the new family situation. Whilst this does happen in some families, grandparents equally can be a great support to their grandchildren in helping them to make a smoother transition into the new family. They might be the stable rock in their changing worlds, the ones they can turn to, who will provide comfort and a sense of familiarity. They can be your backstop when it all seems too hard, when you need a helping hand or a babysitter. So don't disregard the grandparents in your new family. After all, what happened is not their fault and they might turn out to be a real blessing to both you and your children.

HINTS

- Remember that grandparents usually are innocent bystanders.
- Accept that they may be confused and/or struggling with issues of loyalty.
- Reassure them that you want them to be part of your new family.
- Enlist their support.

...AND BABY MAKES FIVE

About two years into my marriage, the thought of having a child of my own became very appealing. I'm not sure that I would have chosen this path had it not been for my stepsons. As I confessed earlier, I was not the most maternal of women. By that stage, however, I thought that since my life had already changed so dramatically and I was doing the mothering bit anyway, I might as well go for the 'real thing'. Once decided, I became very excited by the prospect and was disappointed when it took eight months before the pregnancy test gave a positive reading. Nothing, though, had prepared me for the moment I laid eyes on my very own baby. I'd had no idea that holding my own little bundle of joy would make such a difference. The maternal instinct that had been lacking so sadly before, kicked in powerfully as soon as I heard the first pitiful cry from my delightfully tiny new baby son. It was like falling in love, and it changed the colour of my world to a mellow hue of pink. I recall to this day how gazing at my child made me see my stepsons with a new love and understanding. I suppose my heart was so full of this new, never-before-experienced feeling that it simply spilled over onto everyone – hormones probably had a lot to do with it too!

Having a child with their new partner often has great appeal for step-parents. Those who do not have children from a

NOT COPING?

previous relationship may, like me, want to have the full experience of becoming a biological parent. Others might feel that having a child of their own might balance the scales a little in their favour, as expressed by Rudi:

I've always wanted to be a dad and although I like Amy (his stepchild), I just couldn't help feeling left out sometimes. I know it's petty and ridiculous, but her and her mum being so close, it felt like I was an intruder. Thank goodness that's all changed now that we have Tommy. He even looks like me. I can't wait until he's old enough to come to the footy. We'll have such fun together.'

In stepfamilies where both partners are previous parents the new baby may be seen as the bridge between the two sets of children, the cementing of their new relationship, perhaps even as the glue to hold the two families together. These reasons, however, no matter how understandable, are never good enough to create a new life. Children created from any motive other than as an expression of their parent's love are disadvantaged from the start and are far more likely to end up as stepchildren themselves, as illustrated by Sandra, who told me through floods of tears:

I was convinced that having our baby would make all the difference. I thought that he wouldn't want his kids around so much now that we have our own little one and I could hardly wait — I just can't stand his monsters. But since we have Bobby (the baby), the kids practically live here and I

*am going demented. He (the husband) is at work all day
and I'm supposed to cope with everything – the baby, the
household, his kids – it's an absolute nightmare!*

While the thought of adding a baby to your stepfamily might
have great appeal, it pays to bear in mind that you'll have to
get through nine months of pregnancy first. This may not
bother you if you have been through the experience before
and found it an enjoyable and easy one. For first-time
mothers it could be a more daunting prospect.

Some things to consider

WORKLOAD

In order to care for your unborn child as well as yourself, you need
to ensure that you don't overdo it. If you currently have a heavy
workload, you will need to find ways of lightening the load.

REST

You may get tired more easily and may need to make time
for some afternoon naps.

STRESS

Since stress is not only damaging to you but also to your
unborn child, it is important that you learn to deal with it
and reduce it as quickly as you can.

EMOTIONS

If you are battling with feelings of anger (rage), resentment
(hatred), anxiety, depression or any other such emotions it

might be better to put your thoughts of pregnancy on the backburner for a while.

Be aware that pregnancy causes hormonal changes that can make you feel more peaceful and placid, or can have the opposite effect and make you feel more easily aggravated, restless and upset.

If you decide to go for it, the new addition can have profound effects on everyone in a stepfamily. Frequently he or she, at least initially, is loved by all. Even the most self-focused teenager may be enchanted by the new baby and display something akin to likeable behaviour in its presence, as Ruth discovered:

Having Angel made all the difference with Blake (17-year-old stepson). Even though he was horribly embarrassed by my pregnancy, he just adores little Angel and won't let her out of his sight whenever he is with us.

For the stepmother who is a first-time mother, having her own child usually means slipping into a more natural and comfortable role with her step-charges. She is, after all, a real mother now! This is generally also true for the stepfather. Stephen reports:

The twins are great. Now I just love getting home after a day in the office. To see the toothless smile on their pudgy faces — it's priceless. I never thought that being a dad could be such fun. I don't even mind the other two (stepchildren) so much now. It finally feels like we are a real family.

While the new addition can bring a greater sense of togetherness, stability and joy to the stepfamily, it can also make a stepmother's life even more difficult. The reality of caring for a baby as well as the rest of the stepfamily may come as a rude shock. This certainly was my experience.

When my stepchildren realised that this new creature they had dutifully inspected in hospital was actually coming home to invade their space and compete for the already stretched attention of their dad, their response wasn't favourable. In keeping with their personalities, one child became more passively resistant and insular, the other more hyperactive, demanding and troublesome. With the reality of night-feeds and the penetrating shrill of the alarm clock intruding into my exhausted slumber to remind me to organise my stepchildren for school, the new-found pleasures were overtaken by the pressures of many new responsibilities which, added to all the already existing ones, often seemed almost too heavy to carry. The honeymoon, brief as it had been, was over!

Being jolted into the harsh reality of the plain hard work of caring for a new infant as well as the existing stepfamily can be very difficult. This can be particularly destabilising to the step-parent who was hoping for an easier life as a result of the new family member. Added to the physical strain, the emotional impact of the other children's jealousy and their competition for your or your partner's already limited time, attention and affection might be overwhelming.

The first few months after bringing home your 'bundle of joy' is the time you are most vulnerable. The combination of the let-down after your birth experience 'high', physical exhaustion, disappointment about the children's responses (yet another loss of expectation) is a potentially dangerous one. Enlisting help is of utmost importance at this point. Spouse, grandparents, other relatives, friends and community support groups (such as your church) can be invaluable resources. Even someone minding the baby while you catch 'forty winks' might make all the difference. Life looks so much brighter after some rest!

Having a new baby in the home can be such a wonderful time which passes all too quickly. It can't be emphasised enough how important it is for both you and your infant that you get as much pleasure, enjoyment and fun from this experience as possible. The personal happiness which is likely to flood over you at this time will overflow onto everyone else in your family. They will love it, too!

HINTS

- Don't be too brave – ask for help!
- Together with your spouse, find practical ways of reducing the physical strain – enlist your relatives, friends or neighbours.
- If you can afford it, hire a nanny (even just temporarily). If you can't, get help through community and welfare services.

- Let someone know if you feel unable to cope.
- Share your problems, thoughts and feelings with someone you trust.
- Join a step-parenting support group. If you cannot find one, join a parenting help group or something similar.
- Understand that if you don't care adequately for yourself you will not be able to care effectively for anyone else.
- Know that feeling good about yourself has a 'spill-over' effect.
- Make time for yourself.
- Be kind to yourself.
- Remember that this time will pass.

GRIEF

Even years after I had resigned myself to life as a stepmother I would occasionally catch myself bouncing between feelings of anger, sadness, irritation, anxiety and depression. Although I found this unpleasantly intriguing, I could never quite figure out what caused these inexplicable feelings. Then one day, as I caught myself daydreaming about a number of things I had hoped for and that had never come to pass, I was gripped by an overwhelming sensation of sadness. I suddenly knew that what I was feeling was grief.

One of the biggest issues in stepfamilies is the reality of loss. After all, stepfamily living comes about as a result of loss. For the adult it may be the loss of a partner and the loss of the hopes and dreams for their marriage; for the child it is the loss of a parent, the loss of their security and stability and the loss of their fantasies of family life with a 'happy ending'.

Whether we are consciously aware of it or not, loss incurs a sense of grief. This grief is a normal, although painful, consequence. For anyone undergoing the process of separation (be it through death or divorce) it is important to recognise that their grief is a normal response and cannot be circumvented, cut short or cut out altogether. Trying to ignore or deny it, even though this may seem a good solution at the time, never works in the long run. If not recognised and acknowledged openly, grief will find a way of expressing itself in a hidden form, such as excessive anger, depression or even physical illness. Working through grief is a very important step, preferably taken before embarking on the stepfamily journey, which creates its own challenges and causes of grief through loss.

If stepmothering is your first-time mothering experience, it will mean putting aside many expectations. The partner's time, attention, affection and love will need to be shared from the very beginning of your relationship, whilst the kind of spontaneity that couples without children can enjoy will never be a part of your experience. When a baby (with your new partner) is added to the already existing family, there are more losses with which you must contend: your time, affection and attention has to be shared between your own precious bundle of joy and your stepchildren.

Although seasoned parents are not excluded from the experience of loss, they might enter the new relationship with fewer unrealistic expectations and may feel as though their gains outweigh the losses. Some losses reported by them are loss of time with their own children, loss of energy as they attempt to share themselves around, loss of freedom if their own children have already 'flown the coop' but their partner's children are still dependent, loss of financial freedom, of family intimacy etc.

Children in stepfamilies are often the ones who experience the greatest losses of all. As a consequence of their family break-up and subsequent move, they may lose their home, school and friends. They may lose a set of grandparents and possibly everything that to them is familiar and held dear. If they have been in a supportive role with their parent they lose that role (when their parent remarries) as well as losing their parent's undivided attention. They may lose their own space if they now have to share their room with a stepsibling. They may lose their first- or last-child status if there are stepsiblings whose ages are such that they are displaced. They lose their fantasy that mum and dad are going to get back together again.

While we are grieving our own losses or witnessing the grieving of our partner, children or stepchildren, **the first important step** is to recognise what is happening. Grief doesn't always show itself as such, so this recognition helps us to be more self-aware and more understanding and kinder to those grieving in our family. It is also important to remember that grief is a process that takes its own time. The determination to get it over and done with as quickly as possible usually achieves little more than filling us with frustration, annoyance and a potential sense of failure.

If the grieving we experience as a result of the loss of our partner (through separation or death) is not completed by the time we enter a new relationship, we will find that it confuses and intensifies the grief we might feel once in it, which can substantially complicate the grieving process. This brings us to **the second important step** – to identify what it is exactly that we are grieving for. This may vary greatly from person to person. It might be helpful to write yourself a list.

The following are some of the things I wrote on my grief list:

- Missing out on those first years alone with my husband.
- Having to share everything with my stepchildren:
  - my husband's time
  - my own time
  - affection
  - attention
  - love
  - money
  - special occasions
  - holidays
- Any spontaneity (because the kids had to be considered).
  - going out without major organisation (of babysitters, food, entertainment etc.)
  - weekends away
  - open and spontaneous expressions of intimacy
- Enjoying my first pregnancy in peace.
- The pleasures and delights of having a first baby in the house.
- Growing with my baby into the parenting role.
- Giving my baby my exclusive motherly attention and love.

Your list of losses may of course look quite different to mine; things that are important to me may not be important to you at all. Then again, you may find that some of those things ring a bell with you (in fact, just reading them may cause you to become tearful. If that is the case, don't fight it; just flow with it and notice how much better you feel afterwards). Grieving, although painful, is a healthy process. It's as though our tears flush the blockages and barriers out of our system so as to make room for new experiences, new energy, and a new and different life. So, don't be afraid of grief, and if you have recurrent feelings of sadness about any one issue don't worry – it is common to experience painful emotions over the same issues more than once.

The third important step is to give yourself permission to express your grief. Remember, grieving takes time!

If you are the one grieving, be kind to yourself. If it is anyone else in your family, remember that they need your understanding and compassion. Lend them your shoulder to cry on. Even if it is not obvious for some time, they do appreciate it and it will help strengthen your family relationships.

HINTS
- If you haven't grieved your original losses, do it now.
- Identify your losses – write a list.
- Acknowledge that grief is a normal response to loss.
- Give yourself permission to grieve.

- Don't get impatient or discouraged if you need to revisit the same grief several times.
- Remember that there is no time limit on grief.
- Be kind and compassionate with yourself or the grieving person in your family.

STEP-PARENTING
THE CHILD
WITH SPECIAL NEEDS

In time, it became painfully obvious that one of my stepsons wasn't going to fall into step with the rest of us. If we pulled one way, he would pull the other. No amount of loving, caring, disciplining, reasoning or pleading seemed to make an ounce of difference. He was on a path of self-destruction and, it appeared, determined to take the rest of the family along for the ride.

Although inexperienced in the arena of child behaviour, I instinctively knew that his was far from normal. Largely putting it down to the trauma of losing his mother at a very young age, we made extensive allowances for his behaviour. Eventually, however, in desperation, we sought professional help. This, unfortunately, was of limited success as the real condition from which he was suffering remained unrecognised. Ten years after my first attempts at finding help for him I discovered what seems to have been the major cause of this child's misery all along – he had every one of the classic symptoms of Attention Deficit

Hyperactivity Disorder (ADHD), a disorder which at the time was barely recognised.

All parents of children who suffer from a disability of any kind would agree that parenting these children can be a very difficult, demanding and often distressing task. Depending on how easily identifiable the child's disability is, finding answers can be a discouraging and lengthy process. Whilst dealing with a physically handicapped child presents great physical as well as emotional challenges for caregivers, parenting a child whose handicap is not a visible one is fraught with additional problems that may not be obvious immediately. One can imagine the frustration felt by biological parents who present their child to their doctor, psychiatrist or other health professional with a horror story of destruction of property, physical violence, incessant screaming or any one of a thousand misdemeanours, while the 'offender' sits calmly, looking as though 'butter would not melt in his or her mouth'. In such a situation it is not surprising that the health professional might be wondering about the parents' mental health rather than the child's. Many parents of children with 'invisible disorders', especially those suffering from ADHD, will have no trouble relating to this scenario. The difficulty of convincing health professionals has thankfully decreased with greater recognition of ADHD and other hidden handicaps. Recognising the frustration, helplessness and heartache of a biological parent in such a predicament, it is not difficult to imagine the confusion, distress, anguish, frustration and sometimes hopelessness felt by a step-parent.

Many health professionals consulted by a step-parent over issues that could be lumped into the 'problem-child basket', will immediately assume that the child's difficulties stem from the trauma of their biological family's separation and their subsequent transition into the stepfamily. This, of course, is a reasonable assumption and one that often is correct. If, however, the behaviour is 'way out', if it increases in intensity and/or continues for an unreasonable length of time, one might assume that the child's problems are of a different nature and deserving of further investigation. This task usually falls to the main caregiver. If this happens to be the stepmother, this can be a particular challenge to her as she may be given the impression that it is her presence in the family that is the cause of the child's problem. In my counselling practice, the stepmother of 10-year-old Lucy reported: 'I could tell by the way he was speaking to me, the doctor thought that Lucy's behaviour was all my fault – that I just wasn't able to cope with having her in my life.' Lucy's was incensed at this inference, as the child showed particularly difficult behaviour, which, as it turned out later, was due to a severe mental disorder. Feeling the finger of blame pointed at oneself certainly does nothing in the way of encouraging further pursuit of medical or other assistance. Consequently, those step-parents who struggle with the greatest difficulties are often those who are least likely to get the help they need.

With the prevalence today of children suffering from difficulties such as ADHD and a variety of other hidden handicaps, it is particularly important for step-parents to consider and check out these possibilities rather than to suffer in silence, hoping for change to occur of its own accord. The best way to deal with unsympathetic medical practitioners might be to remember that they don't have all the answers and to keep on searching for one who is willing to support you in finding effective ways of helping your stepchild. Whilst this can be a very frustrating task, it will ultimately prove to have been worth your effort. If your stepchild needs medical help, it is as important for you as it is for them to ensure that they receive it! Most neurologically based disorders, such as ADHD, can be assisted through medication of one sort or another. The difference this may make in the child's behaviour can, for the step-parent, be the difference between a functioning family and a visit to the divorce courts. Should your stepchild's problems be exclusively of an emotional nature, counselling for them, you, your partner and/or the entire family may be the more appropriate course of action.

HINTS

- If your stepchild exhibits problem behaviour on a continuing basis, take him or her for a medical check-up.
- Don't allow yourself to be fobbed off as the wicked step-parent who lacks the ability to cope.
- Persist in finding a sympathetic medical ear. There is an abundance of medical practitioners who deal in

identifying ADHD and other neurological disorders. Lists of these specialists can be obtained from your local Health Authority.

- Be encouraged – medication can help!
- With or without medication, counselling can be helpful to the child.
- Counselling (individual, couple or family) can also be your life-saver at this point.
- If you have a stepchild who suffers from ADHD, it is important that you recognise that the child's behaviour has nothing to do with you. The child suffers from a well-recognised disorder that was neither caused by your emergence in his or her life, nor as a result of your step-parenting efforts.
- Children who are afflicted with ADHD can be helped through medical assistance.

STEP-PARENTING
THE PROBLEM CHILD

Not every child with a problem is also a 'problem child', unfortunately one of my stepsons was both. He exhibited problematic behaviour ranging from persistent disobedience, extreme anger and aggression, destructive tendencies, lying and stealing, to eventual drug use, alcohol abuse and trouble with the law. While I am sure that the foundation of the development of his problems could (at least partly) be found in his undiagnosed and therefore untreated ADHD, the reality was that it made living with him an extreme challenge and a daily test of endurance, resilience, tenacity and patience. I admit that I frequently was not equal to the challenge and often failed the test. Although I tried every avenue that seemed open to me, there were many times when I had no idea what to do. This put great strain on my marriage and indeed affected every aspect of our life as a family. It impacted our friendships, our social activities, our choice of schools, our holiday plans and the way we interacted with our other children. It made for a very stressful existence.

Problem Behaviours

Rudeness, obstinacy, hostility, consistent disobedience, lying, stealing, aggression, destruction of property, violence and many other problem behaviours can point to more significant health problems, but they can also just be the child's way of saying 'I am terribly unhappy', 'I can't cope', 'I don't like what is happening and feel powerless to change it'. It may be the child's way of expressing his or her inability to accept the new circumstances, a misguided attempt to express loyalty to their biological parent, their way of saying 'I don't like you', or a desperate cry for help.

In order to figure out what you are dealing with, it is helpful to look at the broader picture. If, for instance, your teenage stepchild, who has never caused you any significant concern before, suddenly displays rude and rejecting behaviour, the chances are that this is connected with the hormonal changes experienced at that stage of development. If your stepchild's other biological parent has been unable to let go of his or her resentment about the separation or divorce and hates your guts, it would be understandable if the visiting child would be less than friendly towards you. This can be a problem in children of any age, as Daisy discovered when her 5-year-old stepson called her a 'bitch'. She was horrified to learn that 'that's what mummy says when she talks about you'. In such a case it is clearly not the child who is at fault. Emma, who overheard her 13-year-old stepdaughter referring to her as 'the bloody old cow my dad married' was equally shocked though not surprised, as she had felt as though she was in competition with this child from the day they met. Carl found himself at a complete loss as to how to respond to his 4-year-old stepdaughter whose lusty proclamation 'I hate you' was accompanied by a powerful kick to his shins.

In very young children, bad behaviour might signify confusion over the new family situation, fear of the unknown or grief over their loss – this could be the loss of their parent, of their family home, their friends (if you have moved to a different location), loss of the familiar etc. In other words, problem behaviour can be due to all sorts of reasons other

than the child's desire to make your life a misery. Thus, it is important to attempt to identify what the reason/s for their behaviour might be. Having identified them you then need to decide, with the assistance of your partner, what action to take. Whatever the reasons for your stepchildren's obnoxious, horrible and unpleasant behaviour, it is clearly not conducive to harmonious family living. Some bad behaviour can simply be stopped by explaining to the child the effects these have on you and by spelling out consequential disciplinary action you and your partner have decided to take. If behavioural issues with your stepchildren are an ongoing problem, you may need to develop some strategies on how to deal with the various difficulties as they arise. Often, especially early in a new relationship, it is more successful if your partner (the child's natural parent) puts his or her foot down on bad behaviour, thus showing the child that they are not winning any 'brownie points'.

Adolescents

Problem behaviour in young children can be very stressful. Dealing with older children's problem behaviour can be devastating. Open hostility, aggression and rudeness, although disturbing and difficult, can pale into insignificance when you find yourself faced with the issues of drugs, alcohol and law-breaking. While some of the problems you encounter with your adolescent stepchild can be alleviated through special attention, discussion and negotiation, other problems may require a different approach.

Some parents and step-parents who have had children

causing trouble in their families, for example by being verbally and/or physically abusive, getting into trouble with the law, dropping out of school, getting into drugs or heavy drinking, or generally causing havoc in their homes, have found 'tough love' the way to go.

Whatever approach you choose to help you deal with the child's behaviour, it is critical that you and your partner are in agreement. This means that you and your partner need to spend time and effort on these issues, which in turn means that you need to be secure in your couple relationship. It also helps if you have worked out your most significant differences and if your relationship has matured beyond the honeymoon stage. If this sounds like a lot of hard work, you are right – it is! As the cliché goes, however, 'nothing that is worthwhile comes easy'. This is certainly so in stepfamily relationships!

Clearly, problem children are not unique to stepfamilies. I have counselled many a natural parent in despair over their own 'black sheep'. The greatest difference between the experience of biological parents and that of a step-parent in such a predicament is that the biological parents have a long history with their child from which they can draw encouragement. Thus, they may not experience as readily a sense of hopelessness and therefore may not be quite as tempted to 'throw in the towel' when the going gets tough. However, for a step-parent this can be a very difficult issue and can be especially daunting for the step-parent with no previous parenting experience.

Sometimes, however, with all the willingness in the world,

with the most cohesive couple relationship and the best-laid plans and strategies, the desired effect will not be achieved and you may be faced with some very tough choices. In this case, the guidance and advice of a professional therapist can be invaluable.

HINTS

- Don't take a stepchild's bad behaviour personally.
- Seek to understand the child's reasons for his or her behaviour.
- Take into account:
  - the child's age
  - his or her developmental stage
  - his or her biological parent's position towards the child and you
  - the possibility that the child is still grieving.
- Together with your partner, develop strategies for dealing with the child's behaviour.
- If your strategies prove ineffective, seek professional help.

HAPPINESS IS
A CHOICE

Finding no solutions to the enormous difficulties I was experiencing with my stepson was wearing me down. Nothing I tried seemed to make any difference. My problem grew and grew until it was so large that it filled my entire vision. It was all I could think about, day and night. I would examine it from all angles, try to will a way out of it. If a day passed without the occurrence of a minor incident or major catastrophe, I could relax and enjoy precious hours of contentment. If, however, as was mostly the case, the day was filled with one or the other, I'd be severely upset, stressed and mentally going round and round in a vicious cycle that seemed to have no exit — I was obsessed with the problems of my stepchild!

It is a common reaction to obsess over a difficult circumstance, especially one that seems without solution or foreseeable end, but it is neither useful nor healthy. Giving the power over how we feel to anyone outside ourselves is equally unhealthy and communicates inaccurate and harmful messages. It convinces us that we are powerless in our situation and signals to our stepchildren that they hold the power to make us feel, think, do ... (whatever). For the step-parent, this is damaging because feeling powerless, out of control, unable to impact or affect our situation casts us into the role of victim. Being in the victim role we soon become impotent, ineffective and helpless. This, in turn, intensifies our anger at our situation, at the children, at our partner and, last but by no means least, at ourselves. This can develop into depression, which of course leaves us even more ineffective and throws us into still greater mental and emotional pain and turmoil.

The subconscious messages our stepchildren receive when we allow them to dictate how we feel can be just as damaging. They might be as follows:

- I hold the key to my step-parent's misery (!)
- I am all powerful!
- I must be really bad to make my step-parent feel the way he/she does.
- I don't want my stepmum/dad to be miserable/angry/upset with me all the time, but I can't seem to do anything else.

In this kind of situation your stepchildren live in an environment where they see themselves as the root of all your problems. If they also feel in any way to blame for the break-up of their parent's marriage (as many children do), this can have devastating effects. It leaves the children:

- feeling responsible for the happiness (or unhappiness) of others
- double-guessing others' thoughts and feelings and attempting to behave in ways that they perceive are expected
- unable to develop their own identity
- unable to say 'no' without feeling guilty
- open to manipulation
- victimised
- controlling and manipulating
- sneaky and cunning
- revengeful
- afraid to make decisions for fear of failure or of other's rejection
- finding it difficult to distinguish between acceptable and unacceptable behaviour
- unable to draw the line between their responsibility and that of others
- with perfectionist (black and white) thinking
- feeling helpless and hopeless.

Since these messages are clearly not the ones we wish to convey, we need to look to ourselves for change. Easier said than done, you think? Well, you are right.

Feeling trapped in a difficult situation in which you are faced daily with seemingly unnecessary problems can certainly warrant distress and despair. These are natural responses to this kind of circumstance. The situation only becomes problematic when you are consistently unable to shake these feelings; they become your permanent companions and you allow them to take charge of your thinking and behaviour. When this occurs, you enter an obsessive loop of attempting to 'fix' the person you believe has the problem. If these attempts bear no discernible fruit you might get angry, distressed, despairing, helpless or experience any one of a variety of 'negative' moods. In an attempt to shake the unpleasantness of these feelings you may try harder and harder still, feeling more and more victimised by the person who won't or can't change and by the circumstance that you feel unable to escape. Needless to say, this cycle is a painful, vicious and destructive one. So, how can you find the exit?

The first step out of this nightmare is a clear understanding of how you got to be in it in the first place. Was it due to your ignorance of the reality of step-parenting? Did you have unrealistic expectations? Did you think that once you were coupled, all the problems would simply disappear? If you have never asked yourself the question 'Why have I chosen to become a step-parent?', now is a good time to do so. In exploring this question, it is very important to be honest with yourself. Forget the clichés, the answer with which your mother might be pleased or the sentiments you may have spouted a thousand times – tell yourself how it really is!

Professional help can also be very useful at this point.

Exploring this question with Rachel, it emerged that she felt she 'just sort of stumbled into the relationship without giving it any real thought' – by which she implied that it hadn't really been a step she took by choice. While this may be her belief, Rachel's decision (to enter the relationship) was still the consequence of choice, even if she made it without conscious awareness or giving it too much thought. Peter, who thought that his unhappiness was all her fault because 'she tricked me into it', was equally unable to abdicate responsibility. He too made a choice, even if it was rather ill-informed.

The next, and equally important, step is to accept full responsibility for your choice. Regardless of what your answer in step one turned out to be, accepting responsibility will give you back the power – it will put you in the driver's seat! Having taken that step, you are faced with **step three**: yet another choice, to remain in this situation or to choose not to. It is important for you to realise that, even though it often may not appear this way, you always have a choice. In order to illustrate this point, let me tell you about the stepmother who suddenly, upon the unexpected death of his biological mother, 'inherited' her severely disabled 6-year-old stepson. Although she had found his access visits extremely trying, she had managed to muddle through them somehow. She was, however, totally unequipped to be a full-time mother to this child. She felt trapped, squeezed mercilessly by the standards, values and expectations on which she had built her life and which convinced her that she simply had no choice in the matter. Eventually she made a choice to leave the relationship, though only after the daily misery of her emotional and physical struggles resulted in a nervous breakdown. Needless to say, each member of this family experienced great suffering. No one is served well if you struggle through life feeling like a martyr! Some choices are tougher to make than others, and when you shirk these hard choices, life will often make them for you (for better or for worse). In any case, accepting responsibility for the choices you make empowers you and helps you to move on with your life.

If your choice is to remain in the relationship, you need to be prepared to take the bad with the good. Of course, it is important to minimise your difficulties in any way possible. Some problems, however, may not be removable or fixable. Sometimes, the only way we can deal with a circumstance is to allow time to take care of it. It helps, especially in such a situation, to re-affirm your choices by reminding yourself:

- I chose to be in this relationship because …
- I have chosen to take on the responsibility of stepmothering/stepfathering because …
- I choose to remain in this relationship, even when the going gets tough, because …

Every human being is faced with the challenge of making numerous choices on a daily basis. Mostly, we simply accept this as part of life and don't give it a great deal of thought – it happens almost on an unconscious level. The possibility of finding peace, joy and contentment in your step-parenting experience is, however, greatly enhanced by your willingness and ability to look at reality (as it is) and to make clear-headed choices.

The final important step that will take you out of the obsession loop is to stop blaming others or yourself for your difficulties. Simply accept that you are in a difficult situation. Learn to ask for what you need and want without using any form of manipulation. Create boundaries that ensure that you don't get swallowed up in all your step-parenting difficulties. Practise expressing your feelings honestly and without apportioning blame. Remember that before you can take good care of anyone else, you need to take good care of yourself.

HINTS

- Remember why you entered the relationship in the first place.
- Accept responsibility for your choices.
- Consciously confirm your original choice or replace it with another one.
- Do not blame yourself or others for the difficulties you face.
- Ask for the things you need or want.
- Do not use manipulation.
- Express your feelings honestly.
- Do whatever it takes to learn to take good care of yourself.

STRESS AND DEPRESSION

Knee-deep in step-parenting, struggling to fit into some kind of mould, bouncing between feelings of determination (to make this work come hell or high water), frustration (because it never seemed to work the way I felt it should), inadequacy ('I am such a bad mother!') and fear ('what if things never change?'), I was constantly stressed. Sometimes my stress was so great that I felt as though I was rapidly heading towards a nervous breakdown. I was so consumed with everyday life and its inevitable troubles that it never occurred to me to take time out to nurture and care for myself — until one day I fell into 'the big black hole'. I began to wake before dawn and found that I was unable to return to sleep. Black clouds seemed to have descended upon me. Futile thoughts were circling in my head. Some days I felt indescribable emotional anguish. Other days I felt completely detached from everything around me. Occasionally, it seemed as though I was even detached from myself. On those days I would function in a robotic way, *wandering around in a daze and barely remembering whether I was coming or going. I was desperate and depressed – I needed help! It was a very difficult step for me to admit to myself that I needed help. It was an even more difficult step to admit to someone else that I needed help. Having grown up in an atmosphere where I'd not seen anyone ever ask for help, I had formed the belief that asking for help was merely another way of saying 'I am a failure'. I must have been very distressed to take that kind of emotional risk. Help came in the form of a therapist I sought out in utter desperation. Amongst other things, she opened my eyes to the destructive power of stress in my life and to the importance of caring for myself.*

In order to manage stress effectively, it is helpful to understand our body's response to its stimulus. Basically, stress is an inbuilt mechanism designed to provide us with the ability to protect ourselves through either 'fight or flight'. This occurs through a number of biochemical and physiological changes which cause our muscles to tighten, blood pressure to rise, heart to beat faster, stomach to knot, breathing to become faster and adrenalin to rush through our system. Now we are ready to fight or to flee! Naturally, for the purposes of fight or flight this bodily response is totally appropriate. When, however, there is no-one to fight and nothing tangible from which to flee, this response, especially when it occurs repeatedly, can produce severe tension and other serious health problems. It can result in anxiety, illness and depression.

·

What Are the Greatest Stressors?

Stress can have a multitude of causes. In stepfamilies, the most likely sources of stress are:

- unrealistic expectations
- relationship difficulties (especially with stepchildren)
- family conflict
- too many demands
- lack of control
- lack of appreciation
- financial issues

The first step toward effective stress reduction is the identification of your stressors (those things that cause you stress). Writing them down helps to identify them. When your list is complete, do not attempt to deal with every stressor at once, but determine to attack one at a time. Pick the one you feel best equipped to change. Then decide on a way you can achieve this change, formulate a realistic and workable strategy, and put it into action.

Stress Reducers

Physical exercise is a great release for both physical and emotional tension. Studies indicate that exercise causes endorphins to be released in the brain. Endorphins are the chemicals that are responsible for our sense of well-being. Try it – it works! I've found walking to be particularly good. It gives you the all-important time to yourself – and the length of your walk can be varied to fit in with your current schedule.

Relaxation exercises have long been recognised as effective techniques for stress reduction. Relaxation tapes (to get you started) can be purchased in most health food stores and many bookshops. All you need to do then is to make sure that you take the time to listen to them.

Meditation can be very useful. There are many different types of meditation from which to choose, so I recommend that you are careful to choose one that suits your spiritual beliefs. Practising anything that disagrees with your belief system is not conducive to creating internal peace which, after all, is the purpose of the exercise. Be creative – don't be afraid to 'break the rules', and do what feels right for you!

Hobbies are important in keeping a healthy balance in your life. They are activities that you do simply to please yourself. Don't regard these as selfishness; view them for what they really are – a necessity if you are to keep your sanity!

Sleep is of utmost importance. Getting the amount you need assists in keeping your vitality, energy and resilience. It will also help you think more clearly, positively and to keep your cool.

Diet – eating healthy foods and drinking plenty of water (preferably purified) has a cleansing effect on your system. Since our bodies function more efficiently on stable blood-sugar levels, it is advisable to eat small amounts of food approximately every four hours. It is particularly important in times of stress to stay clear of foods and drinks that contain high levels of sugar, such as chocolates, biscuits and cakes, alcohol and stimulant beverages such as coffee and tea. Yes, I know it's hard!

Talking to a friend, family member, supporter, therapist or anyone who can lend a friendly ear can help you put your concerns into perspective.

Plan your day. Being organised and focused helps you feel in control, even when everything in your life seems to be out of control.

Be realistic. Challenge any unrealistic expectations you may have of yourself or of others (partner, stepchildren, friends etc.). Set achievable goals for yourself, and don't forget to pat yourself on the back when you reach them! The more 'patting' you do, the better!

Take a break. A change of pace, a change of scenery, even something as small as a change of body position can be significant in the reduction of stress. It can 'unstick' you and help you see things in a different light.

Change your attitude. Our attitude to something can determine how we feel about it, how we respond to it and ultimately how we choose to deal with it.

Escaping from Depression – The Choice is Yours

Take charge of your thoughts. Isn't it amazing that the thoughts that go round and round in our heads in a seemingly never-ending cycle are always the negative ones – the ones that make us feel rotten? And what happens when we feel rotten? We seem almost to attract disaster. We spill the milk, fall over the cat, ram the car in front of us, bark at the kids and somehow get the whole world offside. In contrast, thoughts that make us feel happy seem to attract positive encounters and experiences.

The kinds of thoughts that plagued me (before I even got out of bed) were thoughts like:

- I bet there'll be at least three arguments between the kids before they make it out the door this morning.
- I'm sooo tired, I just can't cope.
- If they fight over who sits in the front-seat of the car, I'll scream.
- I really should be able to handle this better.
- I am such a bad mother.

I was totally convinced that the mountain of negative thoughts and feelings I carried everywhere were entirely due to all the difficulties I experienced on a daily basis. I was constantly disappointed, annoyed and distressed, and did not realise that the expectations I had of myself, as well as of my family, were unrealistic. It was only later that I recognised that much of the emotional anguish that was my daily companion had its root in the way I was thinking. The discovery that I had a choice in how to think and respond was a major milestone in my personal growth.

Changing the well-engrained pattern of my thinking was not an easy task. It required diligence and discipline, and did not happen overnight. I am not sure if it is the change of thoughts that changes our attitude, or the change of attitude that changes our thoughts. I suspect it is a process that works hand-in-hand, and that one simply cannot take place without the other.

How would it have affected my morning if I had been able to reframe my thoughts?:

- Yes, the kids will probably argue, but that's what siblings do! I'll just stay out of it and let them handle it.
- If I find coping difficult this morning (because I really am very tired), perhaps I can sneak in a little snooze later.
- Maybe I could develop a system that will stop these fights over who sits in the front of the car.
- I don't handle things too well at times, but I guess no one gets it right all the time.
- It's not always easy to be a mother, but all things considered, I'm doing a pretty good job!

If I am able to put my thoughts into a more positive frame, this immediately changes the way I feel about the situation. Note that **the situation does not change!** However, now that I am not filled with doom and gloom, am not angry or defeated (before the actual event), a number of other important things change:

- I am calm, peaceful and relaxed.
- I do not feel anxiety and stress – my stomach is not churning.
- My self-esteem remains intact because I am not 'running myself down'.
- Instead of entertaining reactive thoughts that are focused on negative expectations, I have pro-active thoughts with a focus on positive solutions.
- My self-confidence increases.

This change in thought helped me to like the children and myself better, and ultimately to see my life in a more positive way. It hasn't cost me anything. All I really had to do was to abandon my victim attitude. The rewards: happier children, a happier home, a happier life, a happier me!

HINTS

Whenever you catch yourself thinking thoughts that are dragging you down, stop right there.

Identify whether your thoughts are of negative expectations or are a consequence of past experiences.

- If your thoughts are of negative expectations, consider how you can reframe them. Change your thoughts into something that assumes a positive outcome. **Remember:** A positive outcome is much more likely when you live with positive expectations.
- If your thoughts are the consequence of unpleasant experiences, remember that you have a choice in how you respond. In the past you may not have had any say in the unpleasant situation or experience, but it is you who decides how you are going to think and feel about it. As the experience (since it has already happened) is not going to change if you allow yourself to dwell on it endlessly, you can choose to learn some valuable lessons from it, make some useful decisions about it and you can **choose to let it go.**

Stress that has led to severe depression may require the additional help of medication. At the time, I didn't know much about the destructive powers of stress, depression or the availability of medication for this kind of difficulty, so it never occurred to me to seek it out. I have since learnt to appreciate that sometimes medication can make all the difference and can reduce the duration of someone's unnecessary misery.

PROFESSIONAL HELP

Although I struggled on for many years without any help, I am not sure that I would have survived the most difficult stretch of my step-parenting journey without the assistance of a therapist. Let me tell you, it really isn't a good idea to battle, struggle and strain to the point of total physical, mental and emotional exhaustion that I had reached. When eventually I made the difficult decision to share my troubles and to 'let it all hang out' (so to speak), the relief I experienced was almost instantaneous. For the first time I felt that someone finally understood the enormity of my difficulties, appreciated the mountain of 'negative' emotions I had accumulated and could see the validity of what I was feeling, thinking and experiencing. Talking and crying buckets (initially) about the different aspects of all my troubles felt as though the huge imaginary balloon of distress and despair that I was carrying on my weary shoulders deflated fairly quickly. Although nothing in my situation actually changed (at that time), it didn't take long until I was emotionally stable and strong enough to get back on track.

General Practitioner

Whilst a visit with your trusted GP could be necessary if you have reached such a state of distress that you require anti-depressant medication, the most useful course of action is to seek out an appropriate counsellor/therapist.

Counselling

Counselling/therapy can be helpful in many different ways:

- It normalises the thoughts and feelings with which you may be struggling in the step-parenting experience.
- It confirms that you are not bad, stupid or crazy if you have times when you are overcome with feelings of resentment, anger or hatred toward your partner's 'ex', your own 'ex', your partner and/or your stepchildren.
- It gives you the opportunity to talk (and cry) about every painful aspect of your journey.
- It helps separate the things in your situation that you can change from the things that you can't change.
- It facilitates greater awareness around your issues as well as greater self-awareness. (You can discover all sorts of interesting things about yourself!)
- It can be your life-saver in times of crisis.
- It gives you practical tools to help you deal with your situation.
- It enhances your problem-solving skills.

- It provides you with emotional support.
- It helps you explore your options.
- It assists you in making choices.
- It can point you in the right direction if you require other types of assistance, such as psychiatric help, financial advice, court interventions etc.

Although most counsellors (individual, relationship and family counsellors), psychotherapists, psychologists and counselling psychiatrists are equipped to provide professional service, you are far more likely to get real satisfaction from a therapist who is experienced in dealing with stepfamily concerns. So, without being distracted by labels or titles, don't be shy about asking your chosen professional about his or her expertise in this arena. Your other guide in choosing the right professional should be the areas in which you experience your greatest difficulties. For instance, if it's the relationship with your partner that is causing you problems, relationship counselling would be most useful to you. In cases where the children are the biggest issue, you may consider family counselling. If you feel that it may be your attitude, your inability to come to terms with the situation or your emotions that are the major issue, individual counselling would be the most appropriate.

Counselling support can be utilised in different ways. It may be a one-off support, may consist of a number of sessions or may become a longer-term process. The number of times you choose to meet with a counsellor is determined by your areas of concern, the kind of assistance you are looking for (what you are hoping to achieve) and your financial ability.

Step-Parenting Programs

It is particularly helpful to meet with other people who are in stepfamily situations. Hearing others' horror stories as well as sharing your own experiences, thoughts and feelings is very therapeutic. It's also liberating to discover that other step-parents suffer just like you.

Step-parenting programs facilitate meetings where these needs can be met, where you encounter other step-parents in similar situations and receive important support. Participation in a stepfamily program is usually also more affordable than therapy, and can prove to be exactly what you need.

THE STEP STOP

Recognising the urgent need for information, education and connecting with others in a similar predicament, I have recently created 'The Step Stop'. 'The Step Stop' is a stepfamily support website which is designed to provide

NO CHILDREN WELCOME

information you may need in your step-parenting role, including pertinent articles and helpful advice that is updated on a regular basis. In addition, the website provides links with other stepfamily services internationally. 'The Step Stop' can act as your first step towards finding suitable assistance.

OTHER STEPFAMILY CONCERNS

Money

Finances can be a very complex issue in stepfamilies, and one that can present many difficulties in the new relationship. Money and its distribution are subjects that are rarely discussed before the step-parenting role is accepted, and so can be the object of false expectations. She might think that once he is the stepfather of her children he will accept financial responsibility for them, whilst he may think that his financial struggle to support his children from the first marriage will be eased through her financial contribution. He may be alleviating his feelings of guilt by lavishing his children with expensive gifts, whilst she might be struggling to meet her children's needs or vice versa. Neither will be pleased if they have to make substantial financial sacrifices so that the other partner can meet commitments resulting from a former lifestyle.

This can become an area of resentment especially if your partner's 'ex' is financially better off than you. It can be distressing if your partner's children (who you help to support financially) appear at your doorstep in designer clothes, while you struggle to make ends meet. As reported by one stepmother: 'I am working full-time so we can live – all she (the 'ex') does is spend our money and have a good time.' Steve laments: 'All I do is pay, pay, pay. The kids need this, my "ex" wants that and my partner is fuming because we can't afford the holiday I've been promising her for ages.'

The best way to avoid later disappointment, arguments and distress about financial affairs is to gain a good understanding of your partner's financial circumstances and commitments (and vice versa) before you 'tie the knot'. Discussions of whether you will combine your incomes, how the money will be distributed between former and current family needs, whether you are expected to 'help out' with your partner's financial affairs etc. should be held long before you face these matters in reality. Unexpected expenses may arise in any family (step- or otherwise), but they won't come as such a shock to those who have worked on their financial issues beforehand.

Access Visits

Stepchildren's visitation (especially if you don't have any children of your own) can be a daunting prospect. Goodwill may turn to resentment, distress or despair if these visits don't meet your expectations. If, for instance, your partner's child/ren see you as the sole obstacle standing between their father and mother getting back together and treat you accordingly, it wouldn't be surprising if you dread every moment you have to spend together. This can be particularly painful if your partner seems to be blind to his children's bad behaviour and does not realise how hurt you feel when the children ignore you, treat you like the housekeeper, the 'fifth wheel' or the 'wicked witch of the west'. It can be equally distressing to find your cherished weekend sleep-in (or romantic morning) disrupted when little Sally claims her daddy's attention by crawling into your bed at the crack of dawn. Another step-parent's nightmare are children who make their presence felt by continual bickering and fighting, children who let you know by their rudeness or whingeing that they don't want to be with you, or children who 'hog' their dad for the entire weekend, which leaves you 'out on a limb'. On the other hand, your partner's visiting children may be a delight, may add another dimension to your relationship and be a welcome addition to you home. A friend of mine who is unable to have children of her own, lives for the weekends and holidays she is able to spend with her stepchildren. She adores them and is well loved in return.

Your enjoyment of the children's visits can be greatly enhanced if you refrain from placing specific expectations on these times. It also helps if you do not measure your step-parenting success by the children's responses to you, and if you don't give in to feelings of failure and despair if 9-year-old Jack does not like your cooking or refuses your offer of a trip to the movies. Stepfamily living requires much flexibility and a willingness to accommodate people, circumstances and situations that you would not ordinarily have to deal with. The creation of structure, including deciding with your partner on acceptable behaviours, limits and house rules, often helps the visiting children to feel more readily at home and it will help you feel more in control of the situation. The more swiftly you deal with unacceptable behaviour, the better your chances of successfully integrating visiting children into your existing household.

Setting aside some time alone with your partner also goes a long way toward making weekend visits more palatable. Doing things together that can be enjoyed by all (movies, picnics, eating out) is an additional help.

Co-Parenting

Co-parenting is a more recently favoured parenting option for separated or divorced couples. The co-parenting arrangement allows children to spend greater portions of time with each biological parent. The children might spend one week (or any other agreed time-frame) with their biological mother (and her new family) and the next with their father (and his new family). Whilst this arrangement seems to work very well for some families, it can create disruption and chaos for others. Theresa, who is newly married, finds her partner's co-parenting arrangement, which functions on a complicated time-share system, very difficult. His 6-year-old daughter spends a number of days with them and the remainder of the week with her biological mother. Theresa explains:

It's like a yoyo — some days Anna is here, some days she's not. Even though I don't really want her to live with us full-time, I sometimes think that it would have to be easier than this. I never dare to relax into the pleasure of 'just us' (Bob and me) because as soon as I do I always get jolted back into the reality that tomorrow or the day after I have to be a 'mother' again. Then, just as I get used to doing all the mothering things, she's gone again. The fact that there is no communication between her mother and us doesn't help either. We don't even know if she's been sick or anything. And when Anna tells me all the wicked lies that her mother feeds her, I feel like ripping off her (the 'ex's) head.

Rob reports:

It's far from ideal. Both our children seem to be forever coming and going. Sometimes the house is practically bulging with kids, other times, if it wasn't for our baby, it'd be empty. It is all a bit unsettling really — we just can't get into a proper routine and that's pretty hard, especially on Rosa. She's amazing though, the way she juggles her lot as well as mine. And now with the baby … I don't know how she does it, but it all seems to work okay.

Although surveys indicate that co-parenting is a more satisfying arrangement to all concerned than the system of awarding sole custody to mothers and visitation rights to fathers, co-parenting seems to work much better in situations where the biological parents get along with each other. In fact, the better their relationship, the more likely the success of this type of arrangement.

If you find yourself in such a situation you would do well to consider all its implications. How will you deal with having your stepchildren living in your home every alternate week or weekend? How will this affect your daily life, the weekends you might want to spend just with your partner, your holiday plans? How will it affect your own children, your decision to have more children, your hopes and dreams for the future? Is it going to make your life easier or more complicated?

Holidays

The realisation that you will be sharing your well-earned holidays with your partner's children (especially if you don't have children of your own) can be a real shock to the system. Fantasies of candle-lit dinners, romantic mornings in bed, lazing by the pool with a good book are swiftly replaced by plain parenting reality. Being unprepared for this possibility can cause resentment and discontent in the unsuspecting partner. Roberta discovered this reality when her romantic weekend for two, planned at a carefully chosen 'fancy' hotel, turned into a weekend for six at a caravan park. Her partner was unexpectedly landed with his two children and one of their friends each when his 'ex' required an emergency trip to hospital. Roberta, who naturally wasn't thrilled about this change of events, wasn't at all convinced of the emergency!

If you both have children from previous relationships,

holiday planning not only becomes more costly, it can also present difficulties such as whether to take both sets of children. If so, how do you organise the holidays so everyone is happy? Will the children get along at such close quarters? How are you going to survive two weeks with three/four/five kids in tow? As holiday time is meant to be a time for rest and recreation, caring for any number of children (especially if you don't feel comfortable with them) isn't everyone's ideal. By the same token, holiday time spent together can also provide the bonding experience you may have been hoping for. If the stepchildren don't live with you permanently, this can be a good opportunity to create shared memories. Guy found this to be true on the first, much-dreaded holiday he shared with his stepson: 'It wasn't that bad really, once I discovered that Tom loves fishing almost as much as I do. Actually, we had quite a good time and it gives us something to talk about when he comes to stay.'

If at all possible, you should ensure the family holiday is not the only holiday you take. Spending time alone together is vital to the survival of the couple relationship, so it pays to make every effort toward achieving this. Remember, if the couple's relationship doesn't work, the family relationship won't work.

Family Traditions

Family tradition times such as stepchildren's birthdays, Christmas, Mother's Day or Father's Day can be especially painful times for children whose biological mother or father is permanently absent or deceased. Consequently, these occasions can be very demanding and require your understanding and sensitivity. Many step-parents (understandably) wish to bring their own traditions to their new family or hope to create new family traditions that make them feel more involved, connected and at home in the stepfamily. However, these occasions can become times of great emotional turmoil and conflict.

Sandra made this painful discovery when her stepchildren steadfastly refused to participate in the Christmas celebration she had eagerly anticipated and lovingly prepared. Years later she still remembers the bitter tears shed on that occasion. Sam, although more successful in hiding his disappointment, was similarly devastated when his stepdaughter found nothing but fault with everything he had organised for the birthday party he'd hoped would be the entry ticket to her heart. Sensitivity, understanding, patience and creativity are the keywords to success in this area of stepfamily complication. An understanding that traditions provide the children with a sense of security and continuity is also helpful. If putting your personal stamp on family functions is important to you, remember to take things carefully and slowly. Changes that are barely noticeable are usually accepted more readily and calmly than an insistence that it be done your way or no way at all. Your stepchildren have a right to their traditions, just as you have a right to yours. Demonstrating your willingness to uphold some traditions that may carry significance for your stepchildren can go a long way toward creating emotional connection between you and them. It shows them that you respect their feelings, wishes and needs. As they become more accustomed to your presence in their lives and your way of doing things feels more familiar, combining traditions or taking turns by celebrating their way one year and your way the next, may prove a viable compromise.

Family Gatherings

Other situations that hold great potential for conflict are special occasions that call for your presence as well as the presence of your partner's 'ex'. Such occasions could be your stepchildren's graduations, 21st birthdays, their engagement parties and wedding celebrations. Stepchildren's school functions and occasions of special achievement can also become areas for dilemma. Karen realised this when watching her small stepson's proud performance at his first school play. Since it was she who had fashioned his sword and sewn his costume, she felt her presence necessary and befitting. When she spotted the boy's biological mother seated at the opposite side of the room, she knew that there was a distinct possibility of a distasteful confrontation. She had been the brunt of (and witness to) the embittered 'ex's' rage many times before, so she was not thrilled at the prospect. This kind of experience can be truly disconcerting.

Brawling with the 'other mother' at your stepchild's graduation, tearing out her hair at Amy's ballet debut or engaging in a screaming match at Adam's bar mitzvah (no matter how enticing) does not go down too well. Watching your stepdaughter happily embrace her 'vagrant' biological mother who was never around when the child needed her, might cause your eyes to water (and not because of the emotion of the moment). Just remember, while these occasions can be awkward, frustrating and very painful for you, they can be causes for major embarrassment, internal conflict and distress for your stepchildren. Jeremy still shudders at the memory of his graduation:

> For a horrible moment I thought Paul (his stepfather) would punch Dad out. I've always known that he couldn't stand the sight of him, but it was Dad's speech that did it. I could see Paul getting really hot under the collar when Dad blabbed on and on about my grand achievements as though he'd been directly responsible for them all. I could see why that wouldn't go down too well with Paul – truth be told he's been much more of a father to me than my real dad. I was quite upset by it too, but at that moment I was much more concerned about what Paul might do to him, what that would do to mum and to my party.

Because these occasions should be highlights in your stepchildren's lives, common sense, the ability to put yourself in their shoes and a willingness to forgo some of your stepmothering rights will stand you in good stead at these times. It is my opinion that, faced with the decision to be or not to be present at an important milestone of your stepchildren's lives, the determining factor should be in the interest of the wellbeing of your stepchildren. If staying away seems a more sensible solution, then stay away, even if it hurts. If your presence is considered to be in the best interests of your stepchildren, then let wisdom and caution be your guide. Don't allow feelings of resentment or any grievances you may have or have had with your partner's 'ex' to spoil the special occasion. Be civil to them. Don't get into in-depth conversations that could set you off. Don't give in to the temptation to outdo the biological parent in any way, shape or form. Remembering that you are there to honour and bless your stepchildren can help ease the strain. If all else fails, just grin and bear it.

The Future

I've heard step-parenting described as a 'never-ending season', and I believe that this is an apt description. Although your active parenting involvement will come to an end at some point, you will never know what lurks around the corner.

You could still be accommodating an adult stepchild who is reluctant to leave the comforts of home long after you might have hoped, as Andrea discovered. She had been relieved to finally wave 'goodbye' to her stepson, whose adolescence had brought much turmoil into her life. So she wasn't thrilled to discover that stepkids can be like 'boomerangs'. 'It's too expensive out there – I have to wash my own clothes – and I really missed you!' were his reasons. How could she resist?

Sally was faced with a different challenge when her adult stepdaughter found that she was pregnant and turned to her for counsel. This placed Sally, the busy mother of a baby and a toddler, in a difficult situation. Being conscious of her stepdaughter's inability to raise a baby (on her own), yet not believing in abortion, how could she best advise her? On the one hand, she feared that her stepdaughter would land on her doorstep – babe in arms – in deep despair and begging her to raise the child. On the other hand, worried about her stepdaughter's already precarious mental health, should her stepdaughter choose the other option? She had many anxious moments until her stepdaughter came to a decision.

Other situations I have encountered where being the step-parent of an adult stepchild has proved to be particularly challenging include the stepchild:

- being a heroin addict
- having committed a serious crime and serving a lengthy jail term
- refusing any contact with his father and stepmother, with no clear or stated reason
- being incapable of managing her life and relying on her mother and stepfather to 'pick up the pieces'
- suddenly becoming incapacitated (through an accident) and needing constant care – probably for the rest of his life.

On a more positive note, stepchildren in their adult years can become terrific friends, as Anita discovered:

Rachel and I meet for coffee every week. I would have never imagined that we could get on so well. We used to have the most horrific conflicts, but ever since she's left home we are totally on the same wavelength – it's great!

When stepchildren reach adulthood they often begin to understand and truly appreciate the role their stepmother or stepfather has played in their lives. Bob could barely contain his emotion when his adult stepdaughter, who wouldn't even acknowledge his presence many years ago when he first came into her life, recently organised the most terrific party for Father's Day. He was deeply touched when she made a speech in his honour and was quite overwhelmed by her words of gratitude, admiration and love. There is nothing quite as touching as a stepchild's heartfelt words of appreciation, and any step-parent's heart is sure to melt when his/her stepchild says 'I love you'.

Nobody knows what the future holds. It's obvious that there are no guarantees in life – not for ourselves, not for our biological children and not for our stepchildren. The important thing is not to put off living until your stepkids have grown up. Realise that step-parenting (for better or worse) is a season that never really ends.

THE 'OTHER'
MOTHER (FATHER)

One day it happened, as somehow I had always suspected it would. My stepsons' mother, not having seen the children for 14 years, arrived back on the scene. The older of the boys had just turned 18, while the younger was not quite 17 years old. Throughout my years of step-parenting I had often wondered how I would react to her reappearance and had tried to picture how I might feel and what I would say or do. Now I was to find out.

Although most mothers could not conceive of abandoning their children, some do. This might occur for any number of reasons. They may be driven by pain, guilt, an inability to 'give', share, connect or love. They might believe that in order to find a new and more satisfying life, they must leave the old behind. They might think that by removing themselves from the scene they are bettering their children's chances of adjusting to their new family. They could use it as a ploy to punish their ex-partner, their ex-partner's new spouse or even their children. Whatever the reason, these mothers shortchange themselves and carry the responsibility for great emotional distress and anguish suffered by their children. The same, of course, can also be true for fathers.

Children who do not have the opportunity to get to know their 'missing' mother or father are left to wonder about their roots, their significance and value. They might secretly believe that mum or dad left the marriage because of them – that they were not loved or wanted by them. This feeling can subconsciously eat away at them and, even if they are consciously aware, it can be altogether too devastating to verbalise. Children have no way of understanding that having been abandoned was not their fault. As the remaining parent may neither be aware of their deep-seated anguish nor be

THE 'OTHER' MOTHER (FATHER)

equipped to help them through it, these children may be left to carry a heavy burden of sorrow, grief and frequently guilt. This, of course, is not conducive to the creation of a happy stepfamily. It is, however, the reality that many step-parents have to deal with.

For many years, whenever I thought about the boys' biological mother, I was filled with anger and rage. I was angry for the suffering she had caused her children and I was angry for the suffering I felt she had caused me. I thought her selfish and irresponsible. I was, however, careful not to communicate my feelings to the children. I knew that it was important for them to make up their own minds. When they finally went off to meet her, however, I was filled with trepidation and was wondering where the discovery of their biological mother would leave me. After all, I had been the only mother they had known for all these years. I had cared for them when they were sick, comforted them when they were plagued by terrible monsters and things that went bump in the night. It had been my energy that had been drained in the midst of all the conflict, my support that carried them through their difficulties and problems. It was me who had baked every birthday cake, chosen every Christmas gift, attended every school function. Regardless of my own emotional struggles to do with this position, I was their mother!

The most frustrating and frightening aspect of stepmothering can be the power the biological mother holds in their children's lives. And although I've more often heard this kind of statement from my female clients, it holds just as true for stepfathers and presents a particular area of concern if the 'ex' (regardless whether male or female) operates out of resentment and bitterness. Whilst there are many couples whose separation is an amicable affair, there are just as many (and probably more) for whom this is not the case. It is in these situations that children are often used as the parent's most powerful weapon. Whilst this is particularly damaging to the children (and therefore should be avoided at all cost), it is also extremely frustrating and annoying to the other parent and step-parent, and can be very damaging to their relationship. In my counselling role I hear many a tale of woe and misery to do with this issue which often focuses on visitation, money, and resentment. Following are a few examples:

We go to drop off the kids at her house as agreed and she isn't there. We bang on her door, the kids are crying because they'd been looking forward to seeing their mum and we are livid. All our plans for the day are ruined. Then, in the evening she rings up and asks why we haven't dropped the kids off? She says she's been waiting all day. She's done this a few times now. Can you imagine our frustration? She's totally mad! **Lauren**

I reckon their father should be in a psych ward. I'm not even sure that it's safe to let him have the kids on the weekends. You'd never believe the things he puts them up to. He is stark-raving mad and I wouldn't be surprised if he came after me one day – in fact I am sort of expecting it. God help him if he does – he'll find out that he's picked on the wrong bloke! **Paul**

My partner's 'ex' is, and always has been, a 'vagrant' mother. I've been landed with her monsters as many as four nights out of every week for as long as I can think! She is around long enough to poison the kids' minds, but is never there when they need her. And he just puts up with it. What am I – the unpaid babysitter? I feel used! I hate her and sometimes I hate him too!' **Sandy**

His 'ex' is an absolute psycho! Whenever she lays eyes on us she goes berserk. She doesn't stick to agreements, is extremely abusive, even violent. We moved so she wouldn't know where to find us and have an unlisted number, so she can't continue to harass us. My stepson's handover needs to take place at our office and even his school doesn't have our address. It's crazy and stressful – a bit like being in a witness protection program! **Elana**

What's he ever done for them other than putting stupid notions into their heads? Yeah, he was good at making promises he'd never keep and causing us (my wife and me) one drama after another. Those kids have been disappointed more times than I can count – no wonder they hate his guts. Well, he's the one that's missing out in the end. He'll regret it one day. **Simon**

The worst part is that I can't strike back. Her kids bag me, saying I have a flat chest and hairy armpits when all the while I know that their mother has collagen lips, capped teeth and silicone implants. At handover once she stuck her head in my car, eyeballed me with a distasteful look on her face and said 'I know a good beauty therapist – do you want her number?' I felt like decking her, but I knew that it would make matters even worse. **Ella**

He just disappeared. It's been 6 years that we have seen neither hide nor hair of him. Of course he's never paid a cent for the three children in that time. Obviously he hasn't got a decent bone in his body – the word 'responsibility' doesn't feature in his dictionary. They're lucky they've got me. If he ever dares to show his ugly face around this family now, I'll show him where to go. **Peter**

She moved to the country, stopped her son from visiting us and refused access with the two girls for six months so she would get more welfare money. She didn't care what the kids wanted and really trashed him so the kids wouldn't like him any more. They are just objects in her game.

Ruth

Of course, experiences such as these are very difficult to stomach. It can be frustrating in the extreme if visitation plans are cancelled, changed at the last minute or worse, manipulated as happened to Lauren in the above example. It is difficult when every agreement has to be battled out in court and the visiting children reflect their biological parent's resentment by being stroppy, hostile or insolent. This can make step-parenting, which is difficult at best, a constant uphill battle. It is also a frequent cause for the new relationship to end. Whilst that may be what the resenting ex-partner set out to achieve all along, she or he would do well to recognise that this is neither in their best interest nor in the best interests of the children. From these examples (and I could give you many more) it is clear that creating a civil relationship with 'the other mother' or 'father' is sometimes impossible. Nevertheless, it is a worthy goal and one that can be all-important to successful stepfamily living. If making peace can be assisted by your attitude and by your ability to put down the sword, then for the sake of your new family, your partner and perhaps most of all yourself – do it!

Although I felt threatened in my position by the reappearance of the boys' biological mother, I knew that their getting to know her was an important step toward discovering their roots, getting to know themselves, finding emotional balance and establishing peace in their hearts. I was glad at that point that no matter how tempting it had been in the past, neither I nor my partner had ever spoken ill of their mother nor stood in the way of any relationship they might have had.

Regardless of most circumstances, children usually benefit from having a relationship with both their biological parents. Getting to know the absent parent provides them with the opportunity to see them as they really are – 'warts and all'.

Older children might develop an understanding of their parent's reason/s for taking little or no part in their lives. They might use the opportunity to learn more about their own roots, their parent's background, life experiences etc., all of which could become the foundation for a new kind of relationship. Children beyond the age of 12 rarely develop a parent–child kind of relationship if their parent has been absent for any significant length of time. They are more likely to connect with them on a friendship basis.

Your stepchildren may find that meeting mum (or dad) was not all they had been hoping for. Although this could be very painful for them, it at least puts them into a position of personal choice. Now there is no more need to wonder about the 'elusive' parent. Fantasies of living in a huge mansion by the sea, spoilt and adored by their wonderful, ever-patient and loving mother (or father) can finally be laid to rest. They now have a more realistic picture. This will ultimately stand your stepchildren in good stead and should be a welcomed rather than a feared outcome.

An exception to allowing or encouraging connection between an absent parent and children would be where the parent represents a danger to their children, as in the case of physical, emotional or sexual abuse. Naturally, this is a factor that requires greater consideration if the children are still young. Harboured feelings of bitterness, hatred, anger, frustration or resentment (no matter how valid one may regard them to be) are never sufficient reasons for children to be kept away from their biological parent.

THE 'OTHER' MOTHER (FATHER)

HINTS

If an 'absent' parent wishes to reconnect with their children, the following considerations might be useful. Remember that these are only necessary and appropriate if the child is not of an age where they can make their own decisions.

- Find out the reasons the parent wants to reconnect.
- Establish whether meeting the parent could present any danger to the children.
- Ask the children whether they wish to meet the parent.
- Consider whether it might be useful if you or their biological parent is present at the meeting.
- If everything checks out, arrange for a meeting.
- Hold on to your heart and trust that in the long run this will be for the best!

FORGIVENESS

Whilst I knew how important it would be for my stepsons to meet their biological mother, I did not know how important their re-connection would prove to be for me. Hearing about their meetings, visualising them with her, worrying about their ability to cope should they feel further rejection or abandonment resurrected a multitude of long-buried, painful emotions. I began to have flashbacks to the many difficult and trying times I had faced throughout our journey together. Feelings of anger, hatred and rage, helplessness and hopelessness that I had thought belonged to 'yesterday' re-emerged powerfully. At first I wasn't sure what to do with this forceful reminder of the past, but after a short period of confusion and struggle it dawned on me that I needed to forgive.

Many tears are shed in my counselling practice in the struggle toward forgiveness. Many feel that forgiving is the hardest thing they could ever be expected to do, while some are quite convinced that it is an unreachable goal. While the pain I have experienced in my life in no way compares with the pain of some, I can appreciate their feelings. It seems to come so much more naturally to want 'an eye for an eye' and 'a tooth for a tooth' than to let go of our pain and anguish. Little do we realise, in the midst of our painful struggles, that when we hold on to our grievances, justified as they may be, we actually cling to our pain. We are invisibly tied to the person who has hurt us, our anger and bitterness spoiling every moment of potential happiness. We might spend a lifetime plotting revenge, or simply be consumed by feelings of hatred and repressed rage. By holding on to unforgiveness we actually bestow power on the person to squeeze energy and life from our body, poison our mind and decay our spirit.

With my stepsons' re-discovery of their biological mother, it became obvious to me that the first person I needed to forgive was her. It was important to my internal sense of wellbeing, my emotional health and my peace of mind and heart to lay down all my feelings of anger, resentment and hatred and to move beyond the urge to judge, the desire to condemn and the wish to confront. As hard as it was, I had to let it all go. Only having done that did I realise there were a number of other people in my life that also needed to be forgiven.

In stepfamily living we encounter much that may require a spirit of forgiveness. We may need to forgive our partners, our stepchildren, their biological mothers or fathers.

Sometimes we need to forgive our parents, the parents of our partners and/or other relatives. We may need to forgive friends or other people from whom we might have sought support and have been disappointed. The most important step of forgiveness may be the act of forgiving ourselves.

My personal and professional experience convinced me that forgiving does not come easily to anyone. The reasons that some people find this difficult is the mistaken belief that by forgiving someone they are also saying:

- It wasn't really their fault.
- It wasn't that bad after all.
- My suffering wasn't legitimate.
- If I forgive it means that I am absolving the offenders from their responsibility.
- I was to blame all along.

We somehow feel that finding forgiveness in our hearts minimises, belies or negates our very real experience of pain and suffering. These are misconceptions that need to be uncovered so that we can receive the healing and freedom that will open the door to maturity and personal growth.

Steps I Have Found Useful to Arrive at a Place of Forgiveness Are:

Recognition – I have been hurt by someone's action (whether hurting me was their intention or not).

Acknowledgement – This action has caused me physical/emotional/spiritual pain, anguish and grief.

Realisation – Although I need to take responsibility for my response, the 'offender's' action was not my fault.

Understanding – my painful emotions are a legitimate consequence of the offender's action.

Acceptance – Forgiveness may, but does not have to, lead to reconciliation.

Remittance – I cut the offender loose from my wrath and lay down any desire for retribution. I choose to cancel their debt.

It makes sense to forgive. The offender more often than not isn't even affected by our wrath, yet we might be limping through life, crippled by resentment, hatred and an intense desire to see them rot in hell. Are they worth it? If we continue to hang on to this destructive emotion, who will end up bitter and twisted – them or us? Forgiveness is the key that unlocks the prison of self-pity and the antidote to bitterness. If we can come to understand that forgiveness is really a gift we give ourselves, it makes the process much easier. It also helps to understand that forgiveness is rarely achieved overnight. It is indeed a process in which some days we might move three steps forward and on others take two steps back. When this happens, don't worry, just keep on moving. The day will come when you reach the end of that road. There you will find a sweet reward – freedom!

The benefits of forgiveness are manifold. We can stop thinking about the 'offender' and begin to fill our minds with more productive thoughts. We can stop blaming them for everything that doesn't work in our lives and take back the power we had relinquished. We can pity rather than judge, bless rather than curse. We can stop feeling sorry for ourselves, discover and embrace the good things in our lives. We can laugh rather than cry, shrug off things that would formerly have sent us into a rage, live life more consciously and fully, be kinder to others and to ourselves.

My stepsons' re-discovery of their biological mother was not only important for them, it was a true blessing for me. Walking through the process of forgiveness felt a bit like cleaning the last load of useless rubbish out of my closet, thus making room for all the new and useful things with which I now wanted to fill my life. Submitting myself to the cleansing process was a decision for which I never once felt regret.

It should be understood, however, that forgiveness is not the key issue in abusive situations. For step-parents who live in a situation where they constantly have to battle abuse (whether the abuser is the partner's 'ex', her own ex-partner, the stepchildren or the new partner), the focus must be on stopping the abuse. If you find yourself in this type of situation, I strongly recommend that you seek professional help. Although therapists are not in a position to change your situation, they can help you reach the point of decision where you can make your own changes. They can assist you in devising strategies that may diffuse explosive encounters, find better ways of dealing with the difficulties and provide a space where you can safely vent your anger/hatred/rage.

If this is true for you, don't expect to be able to forgive

until the abuse has stopped, and even then it may take some time before you reach the point of forgiveness.

HINTS

- Recognise the need to forgive.
- Identify the people you need to forgive.
- Work through the above steps of forgiveness.

In order to assist yourself with this process, it can be helpful to write letters to each of the people who need to be forgiven. When you do this it is important that you be totally honest about your feelings toward them. Being completely candid is much easier when you know that these letters are not meant to be sent to the people concerned. They are just tools to help you move your painful feelings from inside yourself to the outside. Don't be afraid of the range of emotions you may feel in doing this. Removing them from your inner being goes a long way toward denuding them of their destructive power. Once written, you can tear up your letters, burn them, scatter the pieces, bury them or do whatever feels best for you. If you find the process too difficult or too painful, enlist professional help.

STEPS TO
FREEDOM

Looking back over my journey, with sufficient distance between its many difficulties and where I am today, I can truly appreciate its benefits and rewards. Let me share them with you.

Responsibility

After many years of being buffeted by things completely outside my control and constantly feeling as though I was doing things that were not of my own choosing, I finally came to the realisation that I had to take responsibility for my own life. After all, nobody had forced me into this situation. I was in it by my own choice. I had no-one else to blame.

Outwardly, and in all my actions, I had always been extremely responsible, but inwardly, where it counts, somehow I never was. Something within me was constantly railing against the injustice of my situation. But no more. I had finally come to accept that I had made the choices, therefore I was responsible and indeed in control – and that was that. Having arrived at that decision, life did not become easy, but it certainly became easier. As I learned to be more honest with myself, I became better able to enjoy my children, stepchildren and myself. I had stepped out of the role of the victim and exchanged it for the role of victor. This, I believe, was the catalyst for change and the beginning of an exciting journey into understanding more about life, greater self-awareness and personal growth.

Letting Go

Letting go of the victim role was not as easy as it may sound. After all, it was the only role I'd known and understood and, whilst I hated it, I was also comfortable with it. You know the saying 'better the devil you know'. The known may be distressing, but the unknown is fraught with terrifying possibilities. Another difficulty in shedding one's victim mentality is the need to accept responsibility. Accepting responsibility leaves us with no one to blame. That, too, is very uncomfortable, especially if that's the way you've functioned previously. It didn't take me long, however, to recognise the benefits of change – no more need to blame, shame, control, fix or try to figure it all out.

Change

Submitting myself to the process of change seemed frightening, difficult and even wrong at first, but soon I was able to savour my new discoveries and appreciate the experience of moving into a completely new way of being. My eyes were opened to the limiting effect of my rigid way of thinking and I discovered how inflexible I really was. Being open and prepared to learn took me out of the narrow boundaries that had previously fenced me in. It broadened my vision and made for a far more exciting and satisfying life than I had experienced ever before.

Compassion

In undergoing my process of change, I encountered many challenges, one of which was the struggle towards finding forgiveness in my heart for the boys' mother. This was accelerated when I realised that, because of her own exceptionally dysfunctional background, she had acted in the only way she could. Not knowing a different way, she had merely been repeating her own history. With little to no experience of love, how could she be expected to give what she had not known herself? Understanding this helped me to cease judging her. Losing the need to judge her also removed the need to judge myself. This shift enabled me to move toward greater self-acceptance, self-worth and self-love.

Love

Love is surely the greatest power in our lives. It can indeed move mountains, change hearts and lives. It is also often sadly misunderstood. True love is not just an emotion, but a state of being usually attained through experience. Ideally, this experience should begin at the moment of conception, should be confirmed by welcoming arms in the delivery room, and cemented throughout childhood by the responses received from the important people in a child's life – usually the parents. If the child feels cherished and special, her needs are met, she is handled with kindness, understanding and respect, her whole experience is one of acceptance and warmth. This lucky child knows the real meaning of love, even if she might never have heard the words 'I love you'. The knowledge of love is built within her inner being and she automatically carries it into her other relationships, which of course, gives them a much better chance of success. This child has a full 'love tank' – she can unashamedly love herself and will be able to give freely of herself. Her love is healthy, not tainted by co-dependency issues, fear or lack of trust.

I was blessed, as I had experienced this kind of love in my early childhood years, providing me a solid foundation and an instinctive knowledge of what real love is all about. This blissful existence, however, was interrupted by my parent's divorce when I was 10 years old. My 'love-tank' that had been full to the brim began to drain, and my understanding of true love became clouded by the pain and grief of loss. So, despite the fact that I possessed in-built instinctive knowledge of untainted love, it took many years of experimentation with everything that masqueraded as love before I was able to return to the experience of having a full tank. Only then could I begin to love myself and others in an unconditional, accepting and healthy way, which is the only kind of love that creates happiness and joy.

Maturity

It is said that maturity comes with age. I believe that the only reason this saying often holds true is that no one can move through life without facing a number of challenges. Whilst people respond in different ways to their challenges, none of us can escape them altogether.

For many years I had no appreciation for the challenges of my life. I hated them, railed against them, wanted to ignore them, escape them, be rid of them. It was only when I accepted that nobody is exempt from the buffeting storms of life and that I have a choice in how to respond to them that I was able to give up my futile battle and begin to embrace my difficulties and see them as opportunities. Increasingly, as I learnt to 'go with the flow', I began to learn the lessons they contained. Maturity is one of the sweet rewards for choosing to embrace the challenges of our lives.

Spirituality

No matter how self-reliant, confident and successful, most people encounter situations in their lives where they are hit with the recognition that all their resources, power, status or wealth are not going to make one ounce of difference. It is often this kind of encounter that moves them into the realm of spirituality. Although spirituality means different things to different people, its focus is usually a power that is greater than themselves.

The discovery of my higher power, which for me is God, was the beginning of the positive change process that helped me turn from daily misery to cherishing and enjoying my life. Recognising the power operating within me and my circumstances enabled me to see life from a different perspective and gave it meaning, significance and lasting value. It opened my eyes to my inner experiences as well as the inner experiences of my family members, and it helped me to see them as the precious and unique people they are.

Peace

With an increasing understanding of myself, in the process of shedding dysfunctional beliefs and with the discovery of God's power in my life, I began to enjoy a wonderful sense of peace, a state of being which I had previously encountered only for very brief periods of time. Having rid myself of the constant internal battle that had been raging in varying degrees of intensity for so long, I also found it possible to create peaceful, loving and harmonious circumstances outside myself. Whilst I have since encountered many difficult situations, seemingly insurmountable obstacles and burdensome problems, I have come to realise that it is truly up to me whether or not I allow these things (that are outside of my control) to destroy my internal peace. In these situations I remind myself that it is never the circumstance, but my attitude and response to it, that determines the way I feel about it. When faced with a distressing situation, I can choose to agonise over it, worry about it, hang on to it, or alternatively, I can decide that it is not worth the agony and the worry... and I can let it go. Nowadays, I am mostly able to just let it go, which quickly restores my equilibrium and inner peace. For this I am very thankful!

Freedom

Having travelled this journey, knowing its pleasures, rewards and deep satisfaction, I am convinced that you can do the same. Whatever your situation, no matter how difficult, impossible or unsalvageable it may seem (or be), and however you choose to respond to it, you too can grow as a result of it. Don't give up, don't give in – remember that step-parenting is only one small piece in the puzzle that is your life. Who knows why it is important that you go through some tough stuff – you may need the endurance you learn in the midst of your struggles for some incredible purpose that you simply don't know as yet. Trust life despite its storms. If you are a willing participant it will take you to your own personal place of freedom, where you can truly say, 'I am free to be me'!

EPILOGUE

When we long for a life without difficulties, remember that oaks grow strong in contrary winds and diamonds are made under pressure.

PETER MARSHALL

Finding myself in the same romantic setting that saw me 'tie the knot' 20 years ago, it is almost as though I had stepped back in time. Many of the same guests who witnessed my wedding then, congregate within the medieval walls of the 12th-century building. The quaint Austrian village, which used to be my childhood home, clothed in a soft blanket of snow, again resembles a picture-book fairyland. It is the perfect setting for our re-commitment ceremony − the celebration of our 20th wedding anniversary. It is a wonderful occasion, made especially so by the presence of our boys.

After my husband and I light the wedding candle (an Austrian wedding tradition symbolising the unity of husband and wife), each of our sons steps forward to light one of the four smaller candles that are part of the magnificent candle creation we had custom-made for this special event.

Proudly considering all four of our boys — every one of them handsome in their finery — I am reminded that my active step-parenting days are definitely over. My step-sons are adults now — busy finding their own paths and creating their own destinies. As I watch the snow swirling through the darkness outside the window, I am conscious that the many challenges that so often made my step-parenting role difficult are now little more than a memory. Of course there will be different challenges that arise with the addition of (step)daughters-in-law, the arrival of (step) grandchildren and the inevitability of life crises. But tonight, as I stand in this same wonderful place where I said 'I do' 20 years ago, I am confident that the experience of those years has equipped me well to deal with whatever may come my way. It's true, I would never have chosen this path had I known of its many obstacles, but it's also true that it's those obstacles that have made me the person I am today.

As I look at the family and friends whom I've frequently missed in the past 20 years, I am suddenly aware that it was the contrary winds that so often felt like raging storms that matured me and made me strong — that the many pressures that shaped and moulded me were necessary to make me equal to my present challenges and ready for any tests the future might hold.

Listening to my husband's hilarious, yet heart-warming speech, I am filled with a sense of gratitude and joy. I love the life I have today. It is stimulating, rewarding and filled with the promise of many exciting opportunities. I consider myself truly blessed.

Having shared so many of my step-parenting struggles, I trust that the message that remains with you is not one of defeat, but one of hope. May it also be an encouragement that the storms of your experience can make you flexible, resourceful and strong, and that the pressures of your life can mould and shape you into the sparkling diamond you are destined to be.

I won't tell you that it's an easy journey, but I can promise you that it is a worthwhile one!

HELPFUL SERVICES

Since it can be very difficult to know where to turn in the midst of a stepfamily crisis, or even when you're just trying to get hold of some useful information, I've listed a number of organisations that are equipped to assist you with counselling, family support and/or pertinent information. Please be aware that the services listed below are by no means the only ones available, but they might serve as your first step in the right direction. Another useful way to find out where you can get the help you require is by visiting your local Community Health or Neighbourhood Centre. The front pages of your telephone book can also be a helpful guide.

Both Parents Forever
39 Cloonemoore Ave
Orpington
Kent
BR6 9LE

Tel: 01689 854 343

Aims to help families with
their rights after divorce and
separation: for grandparents,
parents and children.

Families Need Fathers
134 Curtain Road
London
EC2A 3AR

Tel: 020 8295 1956 /
01920 462 825

www.fnf.org.uk

Helps to maintain relationships
with both parents following
divorce and separation.

National Family Mediation
Star House
3rd Floor
104–108 Grafton Road
London
NW5 4BD

Tel: 020 7485 8809

Offers mediation to families in
the case of disputes, divorce or
separation.

African Caribbean Family
Mediation Services
2–4 St John's Crescent
Brixton
London
SW9 7YY

Tel: 020 7737 2366

Offers family mediation, child
contact mediation and
counselling.

Care for the Family
P.O. Box 488
Cardiff
CF15 7YY

Tel: 029 2081 0800

www.care-for-the-family.org.uk
care.for.the.family@cff.org.uk

Counsels families after divorce
and separation.

Relate
Herbert Gray College
Little Church Street
Rugby
CV21 3AP

Tel: 0845 456 1310

Branches all over Britain
provide specialist counselling
for couples, including
psychosexual therapy and
courses on marriage.

Institute of Family Therapy
24-32 Stephenson Way
London
NW1 2HX

Tel: 020 7391 9150

ift@psyc.bbk.ac.uk

Onsite family mediation and
therapy for families based in
north London.

Marriage Care
Clitheroe House
1 Blythe Mews
Blythe Road
London
W14 0NW

Tel: 020 7371 1341
www.marriagecare.org.uk
info@marriagecare.org.uk

Numerous centres across the
UK offer relationship
counselling for couples and
individuals, including a pre-
marriage programme, support
during marriage and
rebuilding lives after divorce
or separation.

London Marriage
Guidance Council
76a New Cavendish Street
London
W19 9TE

Tel: 020 7580 1087

www.lmg.org.uk
admin@lmg.org.uk

One Parent Families
Scotland
13 Gayfield Square
Edinburgh
EH1 3NX

Tel: 0131 556 3899

www.opfs.org.uk
info@opfs.org.uk

Advice, information and
referrals for lone parents and
families.

www.childalert.co.uk
P.O. Box 29961
SW6 6FT

Parenting website focuses on
child safety and wellbeing.

Shared Parenting Information
Group (SPIG) UK
http://spig.info

Promoting responsible shared
parenting after separation or
divorce, and making available
information, research and
resources to all concerned.

BIBLIOGRAPHY AND USEFUL READING

Berman, C. (1986) *Making It As A Stepparent*, Harper & Row, New York

Biddulph, S. (1988) *The Secret Of Happy Children*, Bay Books, NSW

Burns, C. (1985) *Stepmotherhood*, Harper & Row Publishers, New York

Chapman, G. (1992) *The Five Love Languages*, Northfield Publishing, Chicago, USA

Charlesworth, E.A.& Nathan R.G. (1982) *Stress Management*, Souvenir Press Limited, London

Cloud, H.& Townsend, J. (1992) *Boundaries*, Zondervan Publishing House, Mississippi

Conolly, J. (1983) *Step-families: Towards A Clearer Understanding*, Transworld Publishers, NSW

Corkille Briggs, D. (1977) *Celebrate Your Self*, Doubleday, New York

Corkille Briggs, D. (1975) *Your Child's Self-esteem*, Dolphon Books, New York

Currier, C. (1982), *Learning To Step Together*, Stepfamily Association of America, Inc.

Einstein, E. & Albert, L. (1986) *Strengthening Your Stepfamily*, American Guidance Services, Inc.

Frankl, V.E. (1959) *Man's Search For Meaning*, Simon & Schuster, New York

Green, C. & Chee, K. (1994) *Understanding ADHD*, Doubleday, Transworld Publishers, NSW

Green, M. (1998) *Fathers After Divorce*, Finch Publishing, NSW

Hart–Byers, S. (1998) *Secrets Of Successful Step-families*, Lothian, Victoria

Kidman, A. (1998) *A Guide To Mood Management*, Biochemical & General Services, Sydney

Henderson, L. (1996) *Step-parent Survival Guide*, Gore & Osment Publications, NSW

Jansen, D. & Newman, M. (1989) *Really Relating*, Random House Australia, NSW

Leman, K. (1994) *Living in a Step-family Without Getting Stepped On*, Thomas Nelson, Inc., British Columbia

Lerner, H.G. (1985) *The Dance of Anger*, Harper & Rowe, Publishers, Inc., New York

Maddox, B. (1975) *Step-parenting*, Unwin Paperbacks, London

McKay, M.& Fanning, P. (1992) *Self Esteem*, New Harbinger Publications, Inc., California

Myers, B. (1992) *Parenting Teenagers in the 1990s*, ACER Press, Camberwell, Victoria

Newman, M. (1994) *Stepfamily Realities*, New Harbinger Publications, Inc. California

Noble J.&N. (1977) *How To Live With Other People's Children*, Hawthorn, New York

Parkinson, L. (1987) *Separation, Divorce And Families*, Macmillan Education, London

Peck M.S. (1978) *The Road Less Travelled*, Arrow Books Limited, London

Pritchard, J. (1997) *Stepfathers' Anonymous Playbook*, Covenant Communications, TN, USA

Rice, F.P. (1979) *Step-parenting*, Candor, New York

Smedes, L.B. (1984) *Forgive & Forget*, Simon & Schuster, Inc., New York

Smith, M. (1975) *When I Say No, I Feel Guilty*, The Dial Press, New York

Stepfamily Association of America, Inc. (1989) *Stepfamilies Stepping Ahead*, Stepfamilies Press, New England

Tanner, S. & Ball, J. (1989) *Beating The Blues*, Transworld Publishers (Aust) Pty. Ltd, NSW

Tebeo B.&T. (1993) *Free To Be Me*, Transworld Publishers (Aust) Pty Ltd, NSW

Visher, E.&J. (1994) *Stepfamily Workshop Manual*, California

Webber, R. (1989) *Living in a Stepfamily*, ACER Press, Camberwell, Victoria

Weinhold, B.K. & J.B. (1989) *Breaking Free Of The Co-dependency Trap*, Stillpoint Publishing, USA

York, P. & D. (1980) *TOUGHLOVE*® *Parents Manual*, South Australia